Rejoice
and
Take It Away

Rejoice
and
Take It Away

Sunday Preaching from the Scriptures

Volume I

by

Gerard S. Sloyan

Michael Glazier, Inc.
Wilmington, Delaware

ABOUT THE AUTHOR

Gerard Stephen Sloyan was ordained a priest of the diocese of Trenton in 1944. He received his S.T.L. and doctorate from the Catholic University of America, where he taught New Testament subjects for seventeen years. For the past seventeen years, Fr. Sloyan has taught these subjects at Temple University, Philadelphia. His books include *Commentary on the New Lectionary* (1975) and *Worshipful Preaching* (1984).

First published in 1984 by Michael Glazier, Inc., 1723 Delaware Avenue, Wilmington, Delaware, 19806 ● © 1984 by Gerard S. Sloyan. All rights reserved. ● Library of Congress Card Catalog Number: 83-82986 ● International Standard Book Number: 0-89453-381-9 ● Typography by Susan Pickett ● Cover design by Robert McGovern ● Printed in the United States of America

So now, together, *gaudeamus*,
Because, as sure as my name's Séamus
     To-day's the day
For *homo ludens'* revelry
Ad majorem gloriam dei.
Rejoice then, and as jazzmen say,
     Take it away.
          Séamus Heaney

Contents

THE PASCHAL TRIDUUM

THE FIFTY DAYS OF EASTER

Foreword

The homilies in this collection were delivered in a variety of circumstances but "always on Sunday" and in parish churches — a few at a public Mass in a college chapel. The various locales are given in the first occurrence of each toward the beginning of Volume I, so the key to all the rest is to be found in those early pages. Our Lady of Mercy Church in north Philadelphia is a large structure in the suburbia of the early days of this century, now on the traffic corridor of an urban ghetto. It went from predominantly white to black in my seven years of service there and is currently administered from another parish. The Viet Nam War was on in those years and many parishioners were away in service. Mr. Frank Rizzo was chief of Philadelphia police (with no mention of his becoming mayor as yet). The parishioners tended to be poor, utterly faithful in their Catholicity, and without illusions. In my last two years there, a change in floor plan brought me as close to them in body as I had been in spirit.

I then made a change to serving weekends in two Washington churches with an interlude in Baltimore, in the interests of my social life. "The Mercy," as older Irish Americans still call it, is close to the university of my employment and seven days a week in the same neighborhood seemed to call for a change to make Sunday a day of rest. After a semester's study leave I accepted generous Jesuit hospitality, first in Georgetown, D.C., then at Loyola College, Baltimore.

Holy Trinity Church, Georgetown, has a large number of educated rather than affluent parishioners, mostly white. (Georgetown's traditional black parish, Epiphany, was "whitening" rapidly through gentrification when I served there 1965-67.) The staff at Holy Trinity had several good preachers at the time, among them Regis Duffy, O.F.M., for whose regular but infrequent appearances the pastor added a sentence on the taped recording that answered phone inquiries. Supreme accolade! It was friendship with the pastor of St. Stephen Martyr Church in Washington that brought me there in the four years that followed two in Baltimore. Situated nine blocks west of the White House at the rim of George Washington University, the St. Stephen parishioners included older people living alone on government pensions, Asian Catholics from the lower echelons of the World Bank and the International Monetary Fund, college students, visitors to the capital, and street people. The Watergate complex and the Kennedy Center are in the parish. The church is handsome and the people of very modest means.

A family reason brought me back to St. Paul's, Princeton, a church of my own diocese of Trenton. There, Italian-Americans are the core of the parish and its "mission" (old Mercer County farm families). But a plebeian community (of Irish stock, chiefly), likewise rural in its roots, has lived there for a long time. In the last twenty years executive types have come into the area from all over the country. A generous

sprinkling of international graduate students from the university across the street was a regular feature — undergraduates
normally participating in the Mass in the university chapel
under the vigorous auspices of the diocesan chaplaincy, the
Aquinas Institute. After a year at St. Paul's, which included
hearing the regular preaching of lifetime deacons, the diocese
of Metuchen was created north of the Millstone River. A
newly established parish was in need and St. Paul's was not, so
I repaired to a seventy-five year old wooden church that
fronted on cornfields and a "main church" housed in a
modern, plastic public high school auditorium. These two
homogeneous congregations had an elderly Somerset County
core but they so predominantly came from Minnesota, Massa-
chusetts, and north Jersey that all sharing of Trenton Diocese
lore was lost on them. The gospel, in which they had been well
formed, was not.

   These volumes are dedicated to the pastors who hosted me,
fed me, and finessed various nut letters from angry persons in
the pews. All but one of the priests are alive and active in
pastoral work: Martin McDonough, William Faunce, Henry
Butler, S.J., (*Requiescat*), Donald Sherpinski, S.J., Thomas
Sheehan, Evasio De Marcellis and John Banko. A number of
assistants and an *emeritus*, as free of smallmindedness as their
pastors, made the rectory dining tables centers of intelligent
hilarity.

   One other expression of a deep debt of gratitude. Without
the prodding of Ms. Carolyn Nicosia, and her further prodding of a word-processor, this collection would not have
happened. She did not hear the homilies spoken and this may
have contributed to her enthusiasm. Why she is not in a rest

home for victims of the green screen I do not know. She is the executive of the Association for the Rights of Catholics in the Church, a group into which (from its title) I am too old to inquire.

October 7, 1983   Gerard S. Sloyan
Feast of the Most Holy Rosary

ADVENT

FIRST SUNDAY IN ADVENT
Is 2:1-5; Rom 13:11-14; Mt 24:37-44/Year A

The last two weeks, but especially the week just concluded, have been days of tragedy at home and abroad. The newspapers and television news have given us a symphony of natural catastrophes that have brought on untold suffering around the globe. Death by fire can be traced to arson, to human carelessness, to the complexity of a modern technology in which any number of things go awry. With earthquake it is different. The crust of our planet adjusts itself ever so slightly, shudders, cracks, and there are five or ten thousand dead. The effect is the same in both cases: without warning for some, with warning and experienced horror for others, there is the snuffing out of life for thousands and the pain of grievous loss for tens of thousands. Life goes on somehow, but all who survive are offered a lesson in the fragility of it all, the tenuous grasp we have on life and heartbeat and breath.

The contrast was heightened for us in this country at Thanksgiving by our family feasting, our football games, the character of the reports of the new administration in the making. Peace and plenty, eating and drinking in the midst of widespread devastation and wars and rumors of war, with two men or women literally taken and one left. It was not the flood of Noah's day we witnessed but earthquake and fire and even a battle on the sea. The Bible was scarcely needed this week for images of catastrophe, the end of an old era. The question for believers is, is there a new one to follow?

The advent which we celebrate is the coming of our God. Cynics are free to say that it was merely the dream of ancient seers, all the joyous imagined opposites of a human life on earth that is "solitary, poor, nasty, brutish and short" (Thomas Hobbes, *Leviathan*, i, 13). Yet those who dreamed the biblical dreams and we who believe in them think they are based, not on gossamer and gauze, but on a firm promise of deliverance.

> You, who existed before all ages,
> —come save us in this age.
> You who created the world and all who live in it,
> —come redeem the work of your hands.
> You who did not disdain our mortal nature,
> —come and free us from the power of death.

Like the Jews, the children of Abraham, we are offspring of promise. We have no illusions about life's realities and the nature of the trial. There are in fact the deluded, those who claim that life is all miracle and wonder and instant deliverance in the name of Jesus; but that kind of Christianity is a lucrative fraud. Ours is the older, soberer tradition that accepts the fact that both the fireman and the child are dead, that the rubble before a couple's eyes is the house where they spent thirty years, that everything passes in this present, as yet finally unredeemed, age. But ours too is the tradition of hope that goes back to the first day there was a Jew who believed in the God of Israel. Belief in Jesus does not alter that hope, it only intensifies it, brings it a little closer to us who wait.

Almighty God, inspire your people to run to meet your Christ at his coming, bearing with them the good works you have authored, that they may be admitted to his right hand and possess the heavenly realm in its fullness. We ask this through our Lord Jesus Christ in the power of your Spirit.

Today's vision of Isaiah 2 about swords beaten into plough-shares, spears into pruning-hooks is relieved from folly by its stern conditions: if we let God instruct us in his ways, if we walk in God's paths. As the chapter continues after the public reading it makes clear that the land of Jacob is full of silver and gold, that the haughty and arrogant are running the show —then as always. Yet every fortified wall will come down and every idol perish as men go into caves in the rocks and holes in the earth from terror of the LORD and the splendor of his majesty.

St. Paul reads human history the same way. "The night is far spent; the day draws near. Let us then . . . put on the Lord Jesus Christ . . . living honorably as in daylight, casting off deeds of darkness."

Sings the hymnodist:

Wake, awake, the night is dying,
   And prophets from of old are crying,
Awake, you children of the light!
   Lo, the dawn shall banish sadness,
The Rising Sun shall bring us gladness,
   And all the blind shall see aright.

We are the blind who have a chance to see before it is too late. We are those who can let the LORD instruct us in his ways.

Advent is a fresh start if the stringent terms of the Bible are taken seriously. "Stay awake! You cannot know the day your Lord is coming" (Mt 24:42).

Tomorrow — I mean Monday the 1st — will be a familiar kind of day: at work, at home, in school, in the G.W. classroom. People will talk about the weekend's games, about home visits or shopping adventures. If we stay at home through the day, our favorite programs will resume. At work the workers will work. It will be an autumn week like any other.

But we will have spent today in the company of those who have a lively hope in the advent, the coming of our God.

November 30, 1980   St. Stephen Martyr Parish,
                                        Washington, DC

FIRST SUNDAY OF ADVENT
Is 63:16-17, 64:1, 2-7; 1 Cor 1:3-9; Mk 13:33-37/Year B

"You do not know when the master of the house is coming, whether at dusk, at midnight, at cockcrow, or at dawn" (Mk 13:35). "God will strengthen you to the end, so that you will be blameless on the day of our Lord Jesus" (1 Cor 1:8).

It has rightly been said of our Christian faith that if we were to witness it in its earliest beginnings we might not recognize it. Holiness of life among its first practitioners, yes; mutual support and warmhearted charity, to be sure; but an eagerness and an enthusiasm, even an ecstasy, was there such as we know of today only at second or third hand. I am speaking about a Jewish excitement anticipating the last days that is scarcely to be found in modern Judaism except in some small pockets of Hasidic piety. Christian Pentecostalism keeps the ecstatic spirit alive somehow, but it is the Bible reality simulated rather than lived. The problem there is that history must be set aside as if it did not exist by people who go on living in history. In Jesus' day, even as in that of the Second Isaiah and St. Paul, a whole religious culture lived in readiness for God's final inbreaking action. Expectation was the foremost reality of their lives.

> As when brushwood is set ablaze
>   or fire makes the water boil,
> Thus will your name be made known to your enemies
>   and the nations tremble before you. . .
> We have become like persons unclean,
>   all our good deeds like polluted rags.
> We have withered away like leaves,
>   our guilt carrying us off like the wind (Is 64:1, 5).

It is possible to conceive great religious images with poetry like that ringing in your ears. Judgment, trial, purgation. All those matters become the stuff of life if Isaiah is your bard. But if you have to settle for television jingles, as we do — "plip, plop, fizz, fizz" — or a month of Christmas music to encourage sales, it is no wonder that our souls rise to no heights whatever and our monument will be a thousand lost golf balls. In ancient Israel it was not so. The poetry of anticipation made waiting for God's future the greatest reality in life.

Our holy and glorious temple
   in which our fathers praised you
Has been burned with fire;
     all that was dear to us has been laid waste.
Can you hold back, O Lord, after all this?
    Can you remain silent and afflict us so severely?

Some people read the books of the prophets and it feeds their dementia. Others rehearse the imagery and are nourished in their souls. The Roman Church, mother of all the churches of the West, has long had the custom of reliving what were thought to be the 4,000 years between Adam and Christ in a four-week time of waiting. It is important for us to learn how to wait. Most of us realize that God gives us time as a gift. Do we use it well? I mean in waiting. "God is faithful, and it was he who has called [us] to fellowship with his Son, Jesus Christ our Lord" (1 Cor 1:9).

Jesus taught: "Be constantly on guard! Stay awake! You know not when the appointed time will come."

Sometimes we say impatiently, indeed rudely, to one another, "What are you waiting for? Christmas?" I do not think that Christmas is what we are waiting for in Advent. That, above all, is *not* what we are waiting for. We are waiting for an advent itself, God's advent, and the best sign of it there is, is the waiting. If God were to come — I mean come like everyone else — that would not be God. God is the one who precisely does not come but is only waited for.

The Nativity is a splendid feast. I am convinced of it. But Advent is chiefly about something else. Christmas is not of major significance to children, because in it their hopes are rewarded, their dreams fulfilled. Christmas means a lot more to adults, or can, because it is a time of emptiness, of longing, even — indeed especially — when it arrives.

The God of the heavens and the earth, the only God there is, is a God whose being with us — we call him Emmanuel, God with us — is as much a non-event as it is an event. He fills us with hunger and thirst. He promises in response to our eager longing that he will come. And then he does not come. It is the only way we can recognize him as the one true God.

I speak in paradox because it may say something. To speak in ordinary speech about God's coming is to say nothing.

Yesterday I heard for the first time a song on the radio called *Afternoon Delight*. It could hardly be called explicit sex. It was all implicit — a clever invitation to the young to enjoy the daylight hours, when few questions are asked about your whereabouts, especially if you are at home. It is a case, quite simply, of what Jesse Jackson calls "babies making babies." We have a million-dollar industry going that is calculated to excite, and a billion-dollar industry to abort. It is all part of the modern spirit: "I want it now." Everything on demand. Fly now, pay later.

The spirit of Advent is a different spirit. We want it — the kingdom, the life of justice, the life of peace — we want it fiercely, terribly. We want it when God will send it. Meanwhile, we show our total trust in him. We wait for his coming.

December 3, 1978   St. Stephen Martyr Parish

SECOND SUNDAY OF ADVENT
Is 11:1-10; Rom 15:4-9; Mt 3:1-12/Year A

I pass a Presbyterian church twice every day where the pastor, a cultured man born in Scotland, announces successively on his outdoor notice board the titles of his four sermons for the season of Advent. Advent in Edinburgh or Glasgow? It is kept about as vigorously there as Hanukkah in Beirut or Damascus. For the feasts and the seasons to old John Knox, ordained in his youth a priest of our church, were the devil's game, so much Romish mummery keeping honest folk from the pure and undiluted riches of the Bible. Dr. Ernest Somerville in 1980 thinks otherwise. He has returned to an older tradition.

Yet the tradition he has returned to is by no means all of a piece, solidly embedded though it is in Catholic life. Does Advent mean expectation of judgment, hope, joy, or repentance (note these violet vestments I am wearing that go back to the days when Advent was called "St. Martin's Lent"). Gaudete Sunday with its rose vestments is Gaudete no more with the passing of its Latin *introit*. Neither is Christmas Eve a day of fasting, a practice which confused everybody and led to the "joyous fast." I remember the laden board on that evening my first year as a seminary student — cheese, omelets, salads, dessert, cider — everything but meat. And, sure enough, the manuals of moral theology called it in those days *jejunium gaudiosum*. A "joyous fast" is something like a square circle.

Ask your Italian or Hungarian grandmother, if you have one, whether Christmas Eve is feast or fast. They really did it up right — all because Advent has had every kind of history under the sun. I can remember reciting 4,000 Hail Marys in bed at night when I was in the seventh grade because Sister Edmunda thought it was a good idea. She was born in Washington, New Jersey, but in remembering the supposed 4,000 years from Adam to Christ she could have come from Charlemagne's Aachen in the year 800. For that was the meaning then: waiting, longing.

I repeat: Advent has had every kind of history under the sun.

In our modern secular age which it is so fashionable to deplore Advent is not known to the culture as Advent. It is a sustained invitation to be happy despite all the evidence. I mean that. It is the sole month-long observance we have in all of American life. Forget for the moment the marketing frenzy, the sales pitch without end. I know all about that. I am talking about cheerful music, bright and colorful lights, ingenious window displays. Somebody out there is trying to rouse us from our torpor, our grim resolve not to be caught up outside ourselves. The season is hard on Jews and I genuinely regret that. It has, by way of compensation, a quite secular character and I am happy about that. What kind of false priest does that make me? Not very false, I trust, for I am simply rejoicing that anyone is calling on me to rejoice. About anything. It happens so infrequently! And now it's happening for a whole month. We are being asked to celebrate life in a lighthearted, childlike way. Hardly anybody asks us to do that. Thank God for Advent, the secular Advent even that gets the infant Jesus and S. Claus and Rudolph of the red nose confused.

Isaiah 11, after all, was part of a glorious fantasy. Its author invited the Jews in the days of Kings Uzziah and Ahaz — the final gasp of Israel's splendor — to make believe there was universal peace. It was a game they were proposing but, oh, what a serious game: calves and young lions browsing together, the pole-cat eating hay like an ox and a little child running the governments of the world. It was madness but it was meant to be: an impossible future scheme to replace the wars, rivalries and jealousies that we call a serious and sober life. The central figure in Isaiah's vision is a just judge of the final age. He bears no relation to the little child who is part of the fantasy of the early verses. The judge in time to come is a shoot who will spring from the stump of Jesse, David's father. There is no fantasy here, you can be sure. No one more real than this future great one can be imagined.

St. Matthew thought of this Davidic figure sternly, not joyously or exhilaratingly. That was because he, like Luke, drew on an early Christian source which featured God's apocalyptic wrath soon to be visited on the people in the person of Jesus the judge. Like Isaiah, Matthew is full of warnings about facing the challenge. "He it is who will baptize you in Holy Spirit and fire," winnowing-fan in hand, the grain gathered, the chaff burnt in unquenchable fire.

That, I suppose is one way to keep Christ in Christmas. I think most of us would opt for our secular Advent. There, at least, the cheerful noises keep telling us to get outside our locked-in selves, to rejoice a little while there is still time, to give gifts freely, to live as if others mattered more than ourselves. There is precious little of that in neighborhood or season — the world upside down for a short space.

As in Isaiah's dream.

As in living to the full the gospel of Jesus Christ.

December 7, 1980   St. Stephen Martyr Parish

SECOND SUNDAY OF ADVENT
Is 40:1-5, 9-11, 2 Pt 3:8-14; Mk 1:1-8/Year B

Last week Daniel Berrigan, surely an authentic prophet of our time, was in my city as the guest of some students at the Philadelphia College of Art. In a conversation afterward, a parish priest there who is wrestling with the Advent readings of the weekdays and the Sundays asked him what sense could be made of the ancient poetry of hope-for-a-final-age that marks this season. Violence in the ghetto — the questioner's locale — continues, matched by, one might even say brought on by, verbal violence in the city council and the mayor's office and the school board. At the same time, pastoral necessity requires that from the pulpit there be proclaimed valleys filled in and mountains brought low and the LORD God feeding his flock and carrying them like lambs in his bosom. Father Berrigan said in reply: "The readings are a vision of peace. Without a people who share in this vision, are convinced of it, long for it, the tide of violence can only rise and humanity be even further engulfed."

On Friday in Sweden's capital, Stockholm, there was a ceremony of peace. At it, Isaac Bashevis Singer made a twenty-minute speech of acceptance of the Nobel Prize in Literature. He made the case for the storyteller, the poet. Such are Isaiah, the author of 2 Peter and Mark, Berrigan, Singer himself.

> No technological achievements can mitigate the disappointment of modern man, his loneliness, his feeling of inferiority, and his fear of war, revolution, and terror. Not only has our generation lost faith in Providence, but also in man himself, in his institutions and often in those who are nearest to him.

In their despair a number of those who no longer have confidence in the leadership of our society look up to the writer, the master of words. They hope against hope that the man of talent and sensitivity can perhaps rescue civilization. Maybe there is a spark of the prophet in the artist after all . . . .

In the history of old Jewish literature there was never any basic difference between the poet and the prophet. Our ancient poetry often became law and a way of life . . . . While the poet entertains he continues to search for eternal truths, for the essence of being. In his own fashion he tries to solve the riddle of time and change, to find an answer to suffering, to reveal love in the very abyss of cruelty and injustice.

Was the nameless poet we call the Second Isaiah — the one whose work of genius began at Chapter 40 with our first reading — trying to entertain? Was the author of Mark's gospel? You can be sure both were. The moralist, the doctrinaire preacher of an ideal merely tries to improve the occasion. The artist, however serious of purpose, knows that unless she or he gives pleasure there is no art.

The storyteller [said Singer] . . . must be an entertainer of the spirit in the full sense of the word. . . . There is no paradise for bored readers and no excuse for tedious literature that does not intrigue the reader, uplift the reader, give him the joy and the escape that true art always grants.

When the Polish-born seventy-four year-old spoke of the Yiddish language, his lifetime vehicle of expression, he praised it for its power to convey "pious joy, lust for life. . . patience and deep appreciation of human individuality . . . [and] longing for the Messiah." Those poor ghetto Jews, like the New Testament writers and the prophets before them, knew that "there must be a way for a man to attain all possible pleasures, all the powers and knowledge that nature can grant him, and still serve God." We Christians, like our fellows in hope and longing — the Jews — call that dream of total fulfillment "the days of Messiah." We keep hoping, even though Jesus has come, because we have not admitted him fully. We are in the painful condition of knowing the difference between what could be, in him, and what is.

Isaac Singer said that as a child he heard from his older brother all the arguments that the rationalists brought out against religion. The writer of 2 Peter was besieged by them. "The Lord does not delay in keeping his promise," he answered, "though some consider it delay. [There are some who mock and sneer who will ask]: 'Where is that promised coming of his? Our forefathers have been laid to their rest, but everything stays just as it was when the world was created' " (v. 4). The sacred author says that God delays because he wants to show generous patience. "He wants none to perish but all to come to repentance" (v. 9).

I quote the Nobel laureate for the last time in some of the phrasing that won him the prize. He is praising the Yiddish mentality, which he says is not haughty.

> It does not take victory for granted. It does not demand and command but it muddles through, sneaks by, smuggles itself amidst the powers of destruction, knowing somewhere that God's plan for Creation is still at the very beginning.

We must not forget that it is Jesus' people to whom the writer belongs and of which he speaks. Unknowingly, he describes the poetry of the Advent liturgy. It is not a poetry of triumph but of hope. We live in a world that is literally one of desolation. Peoples are committed to the destruction of other peoples. International corporations grow while heads of families despair of supporting their families. Resort hotels prosper while populations in the vicinity scavenge for garbage by night. The gap of income, wealth, knowledge and power grows in the world today in favor of the "Christian" peoples, as we like to call ourselves. We have mass sterilization in poor countries and "affluence unto disease and pollution of nature among the rich" (Tissa Balasuriya).

The Advent spirit is, indeed, the Yiddish spirit, the Jewish spirit. It is not proud. It hopes where there is no human ground for hope. It asks for God to come and vindicate his own — through Jesus — "the son of a people who [have] received the worst blows that human madness can inflict." It waits on a God who speaks in deeds, not in words, and whose vocabulary is the cosmos.

November 10, 1978   St. Stephen Martyr Parish

THIRD SUNDAY OF ADVENT
Is 35:1-6a, 10; Jas 5:7-10; Mt 11:2-11/Year A

There seems to be a puzzle about this morning's gospel taken from Matthew. Earlier, in Chapter 3, John the Baptizer had entertained no doubts whatever about the one who was to follow him. "He is more powerful than I. I am not even fit to carry his sandals" (Mt 3:11). And a little later, to Jesus: "I should be baptized by you, yet you come to me!" (v. 14).

Now, however, in Chapter 11, the imprisoned John seems to be having second thoughts. Has Jesus turned out to be a different kind of Messiah from the one John had expected —meek and lowly of heart rather than purging the threshing-floor with the winnowing-fan of judgment? Is John crushed by disappointment?

That is an interesting question but its answer would not tell us what Matthew is up to. The real question is the one he addresses to his late first-century contemporaries, which is also addressed to us. Can *we* believe that Jesus is "He who is to come," or must *we* look for another? Having heard the report of his works can we believe in him?

In answer to John's question, Jesus does not give a straight yes or no. He points to what is happening in his ministry. Notice that Jesus, in describing his mighty works, does not say that *he* is healing the blind or curing lepers or giving hearing to the deaf. He puts it cryptically. All these things are happening to people. He leaves it to his hearers to deduce who is responsible for them. In fact, the language attributed to Jesus is the language of Isaiah 35, our first reading:

> Then will the eyes of the blind be opened,
>   the ears of the deaf be cleared.
> Then will the lame man leap like a stag
>   and the tongue of the dumb will sing.

The question for Matthew's first readers, just as for us, is: Are there enough signs that God is present and at work in Jesus for us to believe that we are in the last age? "Blessed is the man who finds no stumbling-block in me" (Mt 11:6). We can, in other words, partake in the blessings of the messianic age provided we do not find in Jesus a total disappointment — a miracle-worker who performs no wonders, a reconciler who achieves no peace.

It is not easy to believe the words of a John who stands at the threshold of a new age because we have never lived in any age but this one. All our lives have been lived in the light of Christ. Our faith in him may not be strong. We know we have the liberty to reject him as many have done, saying that he does not mean that much to them. Yet the biblical view is that John stands at the great divide between the two ages. He is the "sentinel at the frontier between the eons." Ever since the time of this last of the prophets of Israel, any of us who is least in the kingdom of heaven is greater than he.

That is not an adverse judgment on the strong, ascetical figure of the son of Zachary. It is a favorable judgment on all that God has accomplished in the person of Jesus. Desperate as things are in our war-wracked, starving world, they would be worse had we known nothing of the "glory of the LORD and the splendor of our God" revealed in Christ. We say to those whose hearts are frightened:

Be strong, fear not!
Here is your God . . .
He comes to serve you (Is 35:4).

All that talk about violence in the gospel reading, what does it mean? "From John the Baptizer's time until now the kingdom of God has suffered violence, and the violent take it by force" (Mt 11:12). It probably means that with the appearance of John the pace of political-military activity has quickened among the Jews. All the violent men are convinced that God is going to crush the Romans by dint of a bloody uprising. But of course he did nothing of the sort. He sent his

son to preach a gospel of peace, and many found a stumbling-
block in him because of it. It takes great faith to believe in the
works of peace. Anyone can believe in the power of a sword, a
club, a "defense establishment." To believe that peace will
have its victories one must be patient. And trust.

There was a fact-finding team of two clergymen, one
Catholic and one Protestant, sent out from England lately to
Northern Ireland. After extensive inquiry they reported that
the influence of the churches was extremely low on both sides.
That is another way of saying that if either the Protestants or
the Catholics began to pay heed to the gospel they would
shortly have to end their murderous activities. No matter how
"holy" your cause you can continue to carry on war and
carnage only by disregarding the teaching of Jesus.

If we turn our attention to today's reading from James we
are on more familiar territory. There, the wonderful works of
Jesus in the last age are not featured so much as expectation of
his coming. A man named Ambrose Bierce once defined
patience as "a minor form of desperation, distinguished as a
virtue." That is not what James does with patience. He praises
it actively, along with suffering hardship, as the way the
prophets waited for the coming of the Lord.

The prophets were no soothsayers or dreamers. They were
active political figures who worked hard at dissuading ruling
princes from their path of greed and affluence. They foretold
the future, but not by way of gazing into crystal balls or
reading tea leaves. They were more like the French oceanog-
rapher, Jacques-Yves Cousteau, who predicted recently that
the oceans of the world will "die" in thirty years if we keep
dumping waste into them; or like Professor Paul Ehrlich of
Stanford who has made similar prophecies based on the

inadequacy of the world's food supply to feed a rapidly growing population.

A prophet is a person who has insight into the future course of human events based on careful observation of the present, and has the courage to tell what he sees. Prophetic voices are usually not welcomed — those of our best theologians, our peace activists, our strugglers for justice in industry, agriculture, government. The response to such as these is to downplay and discredit them. Yet James says, "Do not grumble against one another, my brothers, lest you be condemned. See! The judge stands at the gate. . . .You have heard of the steadfastness of Job, and have heard what the LORD, who is compassionate and merciful, did in the end."

The Advent season is a season of patience. Not the patience that is another word for despair, but of the careful waiting —in trust — for a Lord who will come. He has come once. In his coming all things are made new. It is we who have been made the agents of that renewal, the instruments of his peace.

Jesus' business was to be inaugurator of the last age.

The signs by which he is to be recognized — that the deaf should hear, the blind see, the poor have the gospel preached to them — are our business. How can anyone believe in a Lord who does no work? But such will be the case if his people sit idly by and do nothing in his name to prepare for his coming.

December 12, 1971   Our Lady of Mercy Parish,
                                                        Philadelphia

FOURTH SUNDAY OF ADVENT
2 Sm 7:1-5, 8-11, 14, 16; Rom 16:25-27;
Lk 1:26:38/Year B

I have been reading lately Sidney Ahlstrom's *A Religious History of the American People*, a book published two years ago which came out in paper in two volumes last month. It reminded me of something you may know which I had read before, namely, that the pilgrims of Plymouth Bay Colony did not celebrate the feast of Christmas in 1620 after six weeks here but used it as an ordinary work day. Their reason was theological, of course. They had the same religious faith as we in the Word made flesh and were fully trinitarian in their outlook. But the Puritan tradition that begot them was not simply anti-papist, it was anti-Church-of-England as well. That church had retained the calendar of feasts and seasons. The purifying mentality in religion derived from a strong conviction about the sovereign majesty of God, the inscrutability of his eternal decrees, and the total impossibility of manipulating him by sacramental or any other means. So the pilgrims worked on Christmas Day.

I should be surprised to learn that any of us had such a view of the feast, no matter how crass we might have been in our youthful dealings with Santa Claus a decade or two ago. Coming to religious maturity consists precisely in discovering that God is not manipulable, accepting this fact, and acting upon it.

The first reading tells a remarkable tale about the traces that remain in every adult to do something beautiful for God which God cannot but take note of. King David's desire to build a house of cedar for the LORD was more than just a fitting gesture. Quite simply, he wanted to possess the LORD, as Moses had wished to do at the burning bush by asking his name. There was another purpose behind David's pious scheme. With a stable sanctuary at Jerusalem, the compromise border capital he had founded between north and south like our own District of Columbia, the peoples of all twelve tribes would have to come to one place to worship. This is the oldest use that power has made of religion. The story from 2 Samuel tells us that God has no intention of being so used.

Such had never been the style of the God of Israel as the LORD makes clear in verses 6 and 7, mysteriously omitted from our reading. He is the wild wind that blows through nomadic tents; he is the dancing flame on the burning bush. All through the Israelites' wanderings from Egypt to the present the LORD had gone about in a tent under cloth. He was the God of gypsies, Bedouins, drifters. A house of cedar indeed! He makes clear that he never asked for one. And David was not about to put the question through Nathan whether he wanted one.

But the story has a neat twist, like the whole biblical record of God's dealings with us. It uses the word "house" in a twofold sense: not only a house of cedar such as David dwelt in, or a temple of stone like the one Solomon would erect, but a line of flesh, a dynasty, that would stand firm forever.

Human beings think of one kind of religious stability — a location, a site, an edifice. God has in mind another, namely, people who generation after generation will have faith in him, who will care as he cares. "I will be a father to him, and he shall be a son to me. . . . I will not withdraw my favor from him, as I withdrew it from your predecessor Saul, whom I removed from my presence" (vv. 14-15). The church has always seen

Jesus in this "dynastic oracle," as the promise is called, and it does right to do so. But the line does not end with Jesus. It comes down through you and me and your children's children through a thousand generations. Dynasties come and go, temples of religion, religious orders, emphases in Christian piety. There is no need that any of them survive. But families and communities of believers in God and his Christ — that is another matter. "Let it be done to me as you say," said Mary. "Let God live in me, in my motherhood, in my obedience, whatever form it may take in my as yet unfolded life."

Like the Puritans of three hundred years ago, we have made our own decisions about which are the fitting signs of the incarnation. We deride the cardboard images of Santa Claus, the sentimentality of Hallmark Cards, the commercial zeal of the department stores. We feel that all the symbols have been distorted. We know what symbols God would use during this season and we intend to supply them. We choose liturgical texts, an Advent wreath, Handel's *Messiah* — in a word, a house of cedar of our devising.

He will not stand for it, this God of ours who is always on the move. He pitches his tent in the most unlikely places — in our communities, in our families, in our hearts. Over and over, in these last four weeks of Advent, he has been moving in and out of our lives. Traces of the coming of the kingdom have appeared in the simple, ordinary places of everyday life. A greeting card comes, a gift is chosen with love, the warm Christmas feeling touches us, and we think that maybe the world is a better place and the kingdom is a bit closer. But then that sly Bedouin slips away — he cannot stand being confined to one place — and we are not sure, not sure; at least, not this year.

Mary said yes, let it be done. You might think that with a baby in her womb, the child of promise, she had him fast. He grew to manhood and went out and died. Mary was never sure.

December 21, 1975   Loyola College Chapel,
                                                    Baltimore, MD

FOURTH SUNDAY OF ADVENT
Mi 5:1-4; Heb 10:5-10; Lk 1:39-45/Year C

One summer's day about ten years ago I drove a small Turkish Ford from Izmir to Assos and back. It was about a hundred miles each way. Pergamon, with its ancient healing shrine to the god Asklepios, was the first stop. Then came Edremit, ancient Adrymittium which figures in the Acts of the Apostles, a handsome port city on a gulf of the same name. I wanted to get to the ruins of ancient Ilium or Troy but the distance made that impossible. I would have settled for Troas, just south of it, from which Paul set sail to bring the gospel to Europe. Do you remember his dream in the book of Acts, in which he heard a voice saying to him, "Come over to Macedonia and help us"? Anyway, I ran out of daylight and was afraid to break an axle on the side roads leading out to the sea, so at Assos I turned back.

I shall never forget the ride home. It was the coastal road along the Mediterranean but there were no highway lights. It was pitch black. At regular intervals in the dark my headlights would pick up large flocks of sheep grazing along the roadside and, standing at the alert, their staffs in hand, would be shepherds as if it were broad daylight and not 1:00 or 2:00 A.M. The thought struck me forcibly that night: "It is not mythical. They really do tend them. The figure of a shepherd's constant care is as authentic as any figure of speech ever devised."

Today's first reading from Micah is in praise of King David. He came from Bethlehem-Ephratha — the tiniest of towns —which should fade into eclipse "until the time/when she who is to give birth has borne" (v. 2). In other words, what it had done once it could do again, namely, produce a great one to consolidate the children of Israel. "His greatness shall reach to the ends of the earth;/he shall be peace" (vv. 3, 4). The "seven shepherds" and "eight men of royal rank" are the bold defenders of Israel against Assyria, the numerical progression being a literary device to indicate a show of strength.

Two summers ago I took an Arab bus from Jerusalem to Hebron, the burial place of the patriarchs Abraham, Isaac, and Jacob along with Sarah and Rebekah. An early stop was Bethlehem, David's city. Just south of it the bus stopped at a public fountain along the road, where people got out to fill their plastic bottles. A flock of sheep happened to be there, refreshing themselves in the tub beneath the pipe that emerged from concrete. In fact, the bus went on beyond Hebron, all the way to Beersheba in the Negev, the southern desert. When I got there I tried to look up a friend from Brooklyn, but he was off doing his summer army service as a new Israeli. So I came back, this time on government transport — a modern bus, filled with young Israeli men and women in army uniform, their rifles at their sides. My seatmate asked to read my copy of *Time,* bought in the bus station at Hebron that has seen so many terrorist bombings. It was hard to put together in one's mind the peaceful, pastoral scene of early afternoon at the roadside spring and now these armed youths — in from encampments where they had no wish to serve, in the midst of a people who knew them as oppressors not liberators.

The afternoon was a parable to me of our unsettled times — no doubt of all times everywhere. There were the occupied and the occupiers from an Arab perspective, or the fulfillment of the dream of Micah from an Israeli perspective. The land had been, at long last, regained. The tombs of the patriarchs —a mosque from the seventh century onwards — were now crowded with Jewish pilgrims from around the world. The fragile peace is kept everywhere with rifles — by young people who would rather be doing anything else, restraining the local population who would prefer to have them anywhere else.

So when we hear proclaimed by Micah someone whose "greatness shall reach to the end of the earth . . . standing firm and shepherding his flock," and identify him in faith as "the fruit of [Mary's] womb," we must know how fragile is the peace he came to bring. The reasons lie in something hinted at in the reading from Hebrews. "I have come to do your will, O God," says Jesus, quoting the words of the psalm (40) of David.

Most people and nations do not come to do God's will but to do their own — to dominate, to subjugate, to exercise power — and so there is no peace. Sometimes it is done with a memo, a glance, a crozier, not always a machine gun, but it is the will to subdue others nonetheless, to have them do your will as it has been revealed to you.

The season is upon us when we need to look within and see whether, like Jesus, we come to do the Father's will in everything. Or do we rather, in the little world around us, impede the possibility of peace?

December 19, 1982   St. James Church, Rocky Hill, NJ

THE CHRISTMAS SEASON

CHRISTMAS
Mass at Dawn: Is 62:11-12; Ti 3:4-7; Lk 2:15-20/Year C

A young woman friend of mine, a Jew who was not raised Jewish, said the other day, speaking of Christmas: "What does it mean that everybody's saved? I don't feel saved. Why do they call Jesus the savior?" I did not answer at the time, nor have I yet. It seemed the proper subject for a Christmas meditation and since I had not yet done the meditating I did not speak. Clearly, a doctrinal answer out of the Bible or the creeds and councils was not being asked for, but a sense in which the affirmation that Christ was savior was true *for her.* I thought I knew, but I did not wish to speak without reflection.

Since then, reading a modern novel called *The Needle's Eye,* I came on this quotation from John Bunyan's *Grace Abounding to the Chief of Sinners*:

> Now I blessed the condition of the dog and the toad, and counted the estate of everything that God had made far better than this dreadful state of mine and such as my companions

was: yea, gladly would I have been in the condition of a dog or horse, for I knew they had no soul to perish under the everlasting weights of hell for sin, as mine was like to do. . . . I saw this, felt this, and was broken to pieces with it . . . and after long musing, I lifted up my head, but methought I saw as if the sun that shineth in the very heavens did grudge to give light, and as if the very stones in the street, and tiles upon the houses did bend themselves against me; methought they all combined together to banish me out of the world; I was unfit to dwell among them. Oh, how happy now, was every creature over what I was; for they stood fast and kept their station, but I was gone and lost.

Now that is great English rhetoric but it is not especially good theology. It reflects the introspection, the guilt, and shame of the late middle ages that gave us Thomas Kempis and Luther and Calvin and Ignatius of Loyola. John Bunyan's sentiments bear little relation to those of St. Paul, who had a very robust conscience. He never charged himself with any sins but one — persecuting the church of God. Neither do these thoughts of Bunyan resemble the teachings of Jesus, who is never quoted in the gospels as looking within, picking himself apart, or reckoning himself a worm before God. Quite to the contrary, the only Jesus reported on had a very healthy self-image. He believed in human sin all right: chiefly hypocrisy and slander and greed. But he never acted crushed under the weight of sin, nor did he invite others to do so.

It can only be concluded that the kind of Christianity that has put its stamp on our age — and the Christian teachers I mentioned are still very much with us — has little appeal for half the population like my young friend, and great appeal for the other half. That other half wallows in its superiority.

But I do want the salvation that Jesus brought — want it with all my heart — and cheerfully do celebrate it on the Christmas feast that is its inaugural.

What is that salvation? What child is this that we attribute it to him?

It is, says St. Matthew, "Emmanuel" — the mystery of God with us. It is a God so with us in love that the enemies of our happiness are undone. It is the conquest of sin — which is basically injustice — by him we call the just one. It is an invitation to life by one who knew that the God he called Father had called humanity to life and not a living death.

I am absolutely convinced that Jesus is the savior because I think I know what the evangelists mean by that, and Paul when he calls him the Lord. They are speaking of a call by God, issued through Jesus, to live as his children — to be human as human beings ought to be. Jesus himself was such a one; uniquely, we Christians say. He did the Father's will perfectly. But it was not meant to end there. Through his agency and power — not just his example or call — he shifted the balance of the ages from a humanity set against God to one that serves God by accepting the love held out to it.

As to the mystery of iniquity, the power of sin, I do not understand it. My own puny sins, yes, perhaps. They are rooted in selfishness, weakness, failure to trust. In a sense, too, they are unimportant — certainly not deserving of the symphonic treatment John Bunyan gave them.

But sin, that mysterious, evil force I cannot comprehend, is terribly important and is vanquished by grace, the very self-giving of God. Of this grace, God self-given, Jesus Christ is the great and unmistakable sign.

There are struggles abroad in the Catholic theological world these days, struggles one can read about in the press. Some teachers say that others are not teaching rightly about Jesus Christ as son of God and savior. Those charged deny it. It is, I assure you, a matter of emphasis on both sides, not of right and wrong faith. The problem turns, as it will until Gabriel blows, on how God and man are joined in the person of Jesus Christ. Some will always say: It is the godhead that matters. Do you believe him to be the eternal Word conjoined to an individual humanity or not? And others will always say: It is supremely important to us how eternal godhead becomes our possession in this man. Neither side understands the mystery. Both are trying to say — those under siege in a more New Testament-like way, those on the attack in a philosophically developed, fifth century way — that Jesus Christ is indeed God with us.

The question remains: "What does it mean that everybody's saved? I don't feel saved." It means that everyone is beloved of God. There are no exceptions. There is none so evil or so warped as to escape the power of this love, though some seem to resist it. God did not begin to love his children with the birth of Jesus, nor does he confine his love to those who confess Jesus' name. He is not a God so limited as that. His love, his justice is everywhere and available to all. But something did happen in history one Palestinian night and with the birth of this child of Mary, this Jew, there was a watershed in the power of sin over humanity. We no longer need live in anxiety or fear. We can live in love.

Salvation may not be the best word. Because we have all but ruined it, it may no longer be a good phrase, yet we continue to proclaim it: "There is born to you a savior who is

Christ the Lord" (Lk 2:11). And "You shall call his name Jesus, because he will save the people from their sins" (Mt 1:21), from becoming their own worst selves.

December 25, 1979   St. Stephen Martyr Parish

CHRISTMAS
Mass during the Day: Is 52:7-10, Heb 1:1-6; Jn 1:1-18/Year B

Break out together in song,
  O ruins of Jerusalem!
for the LORD comforts his people,
  he redeems Jerusalem.
the LORD has bared his holy arm
  in the sight of all the nations;
all the ends of the earth will behold
  the salvation of our God. (vv. 9f.)

This is the poetry of an accomplished fact. Peace, salvation, all these things have come to holy Zion in the restoration of Israel from Babylonian exile. Watchmen on the city walls have hailed the people's return — their *aliyah*, as the Israelis still call such a return-for-life. God has done a work of power in the sight of the nations, the literal saving of his people. We Christians take this poetry and apply it to Jesus' birth: God's speaking to us through his son in this, the first stage of the final age.

Have you noticed, in listening to the English carols — most of them pre-Reformation except *Adeste Fideles* and the American *O Little Town of Bethlehem* — how recurrent are the words joy, jolly, merry, gladness, cheer? This was no accident, even though the songs came out of an age marked by as much tragedy and sorrow as our own. It was part of the Catholic thought of the times, the conviction that God had wrought a work that literally changed human lives. The Reformation with its heavy emphasis on introspection came to have another view. The human creature was a sinner, as much after the birth of Jesus as before. Humanity deserved death in punishment and was set on the road to salvation only by the gratuitous mercy of God. The redemption was a marvel, some strains of Reformation thought had it, but in fact it changed nothing; God merely looked upon his loathsome creature as now accepted. That is why the early Calvinists and various Anabaptists — though not the Lutherans — looked on Christmas as no different from any other day. They termed celebrating it as idolatrous, a reliance on feasts and seasons forbidden by Galatians 4:10 and not on the saving mercy that overlooked our transgressions.

We Catholics were and are in a different tradition in all this. Like the Jews returning from exile we think that God has done a deed that makes a difference *in us.* He does not merely accept us graciously — totally unchanged. God changes us into the image of his son, or will if we permit it. And so we feast and make merry, we eat and drink more than we need to, we exchange presents and visit family, not in a spirit of ancient paganism but in a spirit of renewal — yearly newness in a child's birth. "This means that if anyone is in Christ that person is a new creation. The old order has passed away. Now all is new! All this has been done by God who has reconciled us to himself through Christ and has given us the ministry of reconciliation" (2 Cor 5:17-19). So that, on Christmas Day, when we bid one another be merry we mean it from the heart. There is *reason* for merriment. We are a people made new.

This semester I taught a course to graduate students called "Introduction to Christianity." Enrolled in it were eleven American Jews and one Israeli, three Muslims (two Pakistani men and a woman from Khartoum in Sudan) and two Christians, a Protestant and a Catholic. We read the New Testament, selections from the church fathers, Anselm and Aquinas, Luther and Calvin, Tillich and Rahner. I have just finished grading the exams. They were a brainy bunch, so it was a pleasure to read what they wrote. It was rewarding to see the non-Christians especially get the mysteries of the incarnation and redemption straight, in page after page of flawless history and theology. But they had had to lay many previous misconceptions aside, they told me. Where did they get them? From growing up among Christians in America. Or from reading books by other non-Christians that explained Christianity to them.

Thus, it came as a great surprise to most to learn that Christians take the human status of Jesus seriously. Muslims and Jews alike thought that our faith is that he is God in human form, indeed that Jesus is God to us in exactly the way that God is God to them. It came as a great surprise to them to learn that we attribute everything to God, the origin and source of all, just as Jesus did. Further — and this shows the influence of Reformation teaching all around the globe —they supposed almost universally that Christianity teaches that a correlate of the power of God in the work of salvation is the powerlessness of humanity. Christianity for them is a religion that conceives our race as so sinful that it is capable of nothing. It is passive, helpless, in need of an assistance from God in which it plays no part whatever.

But that is not the Christianity we celebrate today. Christmas is a feast of humanity respected, empowered, indwelt by God. In bringing to birth his son as one of us, God has told us all that he means us to be. As a French churchman of the 17th century, Cardinal Bérulle, once wrote: "He has entrusted us to ourselves." This assigns to our freedom the duty of making the kingdom — God's perfect rule over us — come. That is why any downgrading of liberty on the part of Christians — it is also a Catholic vice — far from serving the cause of God reduces faith to a habit or to conformity. It may parade as an exalted reliance on God for everything, but it shortly has little to do with human hopes and burdens. We do not pretend to compete with the Creator but we fulfill the teaching of God's son by encouraging the maximum liberty and the maximum social communication — at our best as Catholics, that is.

And so I bid you, "God rest ye merry, gentlewomen, gentlemen." The state of things is different with us because of this day. We celebrate a child who was born free and who gave us back the gift his Father would never have had us lose, our freedom. It is not a freedom to judge so as to deprive of livelihood, to kill, to enslave or torture anyone, whether it be the church that claim it or the civil arm. It is the freedom to be a person like the divine person, like deity itself. "The personality is the special vision that each one has of God."

We look into the crib and see there not only the one that Jesus was called to be but the one that we are called to be.

Joy, jollity, merriment, gladness? There is indeed every reason for it under the winter sun.

December 25, 1978   St. Stephen Martyr Parish

FEAST OF THE HOLY FAMILY
Sir 3:2-6, 12-14; Col 3:12-21; Lk 2:22-40/Year B

Christmas is a great family feast, even in our secular society. At this season all flights are booked, bus and train stations and highways are crowded, yesterday long distance telephone lines were humming steadily. The celebration of Christmas, of the incarnation of God's word among us, has made *this* difference: that even those who are not believers or followers of Jesus take time to renew and strengthen family ties. Bonds of affection are tightened; personal caring and fidelity are examined anew. Committed Christians in particular tend to know the reasons for their family joy.

It does not always work that way, of course. The greatest opportunities for good have their darker side, leaving the door open to incalculable pain and suffering. Severe wounds are inflicted on families at the Christmas season — slights and hurts and sharp words that will be remembered for years. It is a time when many family members are simply off the scene — lost in an alcoholic haze. The psychological strains of this time, when everyone is expected to be happy by social mandate, are indeed more than some can bear. I shall try not to add to the burden a few of you are carrying this season by a cheerful homily at this early hour on the day after Christmas. It *is* a time, though, to meditate carefully — not mindlessly —on the reality of family.

Who makes up a family in America nowadays? All sorts of people, of every age and condition. Half of our households have a single parent. There are millions of couples, young and old, living without benefit of a rite of marriage. Communal situations abound — in white and black and brown families — in which the lines of parentage and childcare are blurred. There are households of single people made up of older brothers and sisters; many households of single people are homosexual in their orientation. The sociologist's nuclear family of a mother, father, and children born to them has a noble past and a lively future but it can hardly be called typical. That is so if only because so many children have been born to one parent in a household but not to the other.

There is no correlation, it seems, between the family unit that is legally or sacramentally or morally "regular" and its happiness. The only positive correlation that exists is between the amount of love, which is to say sacrifice, that goes into life under one roof — or in one living space — and the happiness that comes of it. Many "irregular" households, the result of multiple marriage or no marriage, are unhappy because they have mutual selfishness as their cornerstone. But then, many "regular" households, even of the churchgoing, are armed camps for the same reason: there is selfishness at their root.

Today's feast of the Holy Family does not have the appeal it should for many Catholics. That is because the New Testament record of Jesus' family life is drawn on so selectively in the creation of the feast. The nativity story, the circumcision and redemption of a firstborn son, the flight into Egypt, and the finding of Jesus among the learned at age twelve are woven together from Matthew and Luke to make a single story of idyllic obedience. Many a harried mother has reflected with a certain bitterness that it would be fine to raise one perfect child with the help of a perfect husband who was a model of chastity and hard work, gentleness and consideration of others. Many a frustrated father, feeling enraged and defeated, has looked upon this saccharine scene and found it unreal and discouraging.

The total gospel record is much more reassuring in its uncertainties than that careful splicing of early Luke and Matthew allows. Even these two do not mask the fact that Jesus' illegitimacy was an early charge leveled at the Christian movement. All the evangelists, by their silence, suggest Joseph's early death. For Jesus' public career they propose a large kinship circle, most members of whom are unsympathetic not to say inimical to his aspirations. Mark even writes that some of them thought he was crazy (cf. Mk 3:21; Jn 7:5). As to the continence of Mary and Joseph, it may create some marvelling at Joseph's restraint but there are few among the married who can derive comfort from this unusual arrangement. Christian family life must find its dynamism in some other source.

The early verses of our reading from Colossians are not directed exclusively to families but they make a lot of sense there. "Forgive whatever grievances you have against one another" (v. 13). Can you manage it, in this season? Be "kind, humble, patient" (v. 12), "instruct one another" (v. 16). The language is low-key and disarming but it touches directly on the tense situations in families that come from circumstances, not from choice. Especially at holiday time. There is not enough income to meet all the family obligations and children often don't understand this. They bring in another standard from outside. The two sides of the family often have different standards. His side and hers bring lots of pressure, both using *their* family member as a hostage. And why is it that people who love one another must have such a widely divergent approach to practically everything? That is at the same time the mystery of married love and the mystery of the family.

The strains of life in a family, be it a large clan or a small unit, are not easily overcome. It takes courage and sympathy to show understanding and love to a family member who is unusual. How do the non-conformists fare in your family —the teens and twenties who won't go to church, the perpetual students, the ones who don't seem to want a job or like any job they get? I could go on talking like this for an hour. I might even lapse into a burst of honesty and tell you about the pain of growing up in my family — or the void of not having had a family of my own. I am sure you would not especially profit from either development. You have experience enough of your own.

What I know we have in common is the power of the gospel and the pain of living close to, or distant from, those whom we love best. It is at times an intolerable pain. But because there is nothing in human life quite like a family, however it is composed, the game is worth the candle.

And the name of the game is forgiveness as often as it is love.

December 27, 1981   St. James Church

SOLEMNITY OF MARY, MOTHER OF GOD
Nm 6:22-27; Gal 4:4-7; Lk 2:16-21/Year B

Today's feast has had various adventures in the Christian calendar. It began its career as the first observance of Mary's place in the scheme of our redemption on the octave day of Christmas. It has come back to that in the lately revised Roman calendar of feasts. The Christian church has never celebrated the first day of the year as such, even though that fact is uppermost in people's minds and the planners of the calendar of feasts are well aware of it. In the period when the Roman calendar was being hammered out the populace was as mad over chariot racing and gladiatorial combat as it is now over football. In those days, you did not root for Penn State or Notre Dame but for "the blues," "the greens," "the reds," and "the whites." So the contest between liturgical activity and athletic passivity is almost as old as Christianity, and religion is well accustomed to being the loser.

Earlier this year there appeared a book produced by twelve Christian scholars entitled *Mary in the New Testament*. It was sponsored by the U.S. Lutheran and Roman Catholic Dialogue, an official discussion by theologians of the two churches. Fittingly enough, the co-publishers of the book are Fortress Press and Paulist Press, respectively Lutheran and Catholic houses. The authors' hope was to present the New Testament data on Mary dispassionately, though they are aware that they tend to give different emphases to the varied New Testament witness itself.

The role Mary has played in keeping Christians apart is well known. It dates to the second-century gnostic period when Catholics stressed her motherhood of Jesus as proof of his humanity, while the Valentinians held that Jesus "passed through Mary as water runs through a tube" (Irenaeus, *Against Heresies,* 1.7.2; cf. *The* [Coptic] *Gospel of Philip, 55:23.*). Again, in 431 at the Council of Ephesus, the Catholics defined Mary by the title "Mother of God" while the followers of Nestorius favored the lesser title — as Catholics thought —"Mother of Christ." But the great struggle over Mary came with the 16th century Reformers who saw in her a threat to the unique mediatorship of Christ her son. They were opposed to medieval excesses which accorded to Mary all but divine powers, and that was good. At the same time, they tended to deny any power of witness to the church's faith concerning Mary of the church fathers, the councils, and the feasts of the liturgy. Their watchword "Scripture alone" demanded this. Since much of the association of Mary with her son in the work of the redemption was the second-century doing of Sts. Justin and Irenaeus, writings like the apocryphal Protoevangelium of James and sixth-century feasts like that of today, the Marian piety of 1200 years was attacked as an illegitimate, postbiblical development.

The authors of *Mary in the New Testament,* being peaceful in intent, do not argue over whether the New Testament contains the sole witness to Christian faith. The development of doctrine is an important difference between Catholics and Protestants, as it is between the Eastern Orthodox and Protestants. The authors set all this to one side, concentrating on what the various New Testament authors say. There St. Mark, by his silence, seems to describe Mary as one of Jesus' relatives disinterested in her son's message. This may not be historical so much as part of his stress on the "family" of Jesus of the final age, namely, believers in him as the inaugurator of the end-time as contrasted with those related by blood and even those who had been his disciples in his lifetime. Matthew and Luke each has a conception and birth of Jesus narrative in which Mary figures. In Luke Mary is central, in Matthew Joseph is. The result is a softening of the stark treatment of Mary in Mark when Matthew and Luke edit the Marcan passages. John, as is well known, has no birth narrative but he inserts the mother of Jesus into the Cana miracle for purposes of having this same "woman" stand at the foot of the cross when Jesus' "hour" has come. Mary appears in the Acts of the Apostles only once (1:14), among the women of the company and Jesus' brethren in the upper room. As to St. Paul, today's second reading is his sole reference to Jesus' mother. But here as in the prologue to Romans which has Jesus "descended from David according to the flesh," Paul's interest is in Jesus' true humanity and Mosaic Jewishness, not in Mary's personal role.

We who are Catholics, like the Orthodox and some Anglicans, tend to disregard Mark's deemphasis of Mary and Paul's silence about her. We go in an arc from the marvelous material in praise of her motherhood in Luke and her intercession at Cana in John to the second century, when the paean in praise of her role in the redemption begins in earnest.

You hear it said from time to time that the Catholics have kept what the Protestants lost, a sense of the feminine in God through devotion to Mary. But that represents confusion, all ways. Deity is every bit as feminine as it is masculine, being at the same time neither and both. What Mary represents is the feminine not in deity but in humanity, where we are quite skilled enough at forgetting it. She is a wife, she is a mother, she is a believer. She has a totally independent personal existence from role and family. For all these reasons we cherish her. Mary is the great reminder of the kind of human race, the kind of persons of both sexes we really are.

January 1, 1979   St. Stephen Martyr Parish

THE BAPTISM OF THE LORD
Is 42:1-4, 6-7; Ac 10:34-38; Lk 3:15-16, 21-22/Year C

Today's feast is about mission — yours, mine, and the garbage collector's. For all the baptized are "missioned," not just professional ministers. I get the blues a little bit when I hear the weekly prayer for answers to the call to the priesthood or life in religious communities. I know there must be such people. I am happy to be one of them. But praying for their emergence from the parish family seems putting the cart before the horse. If we each experienced our own call and mission more vividly, it surely would occur to some to do it in those particular ways. But if we are generally spiritless as a Christian community, what kind of life is that to invite young people to?

Life and the living of it is our baptism; dead to the old self we rise to pain, to joy, to demands of greater faith and further hope.

Baptism is a process that continues over many years, symbolized and effected by the sacramental sign received long

ago. It is a priestly commitment. To be baptized is to share in
the priesthood of Christ, having a part in the reconciling of all
nature, all humanity to God. The Christian is a mediatorial
person, one who offers body, blood, and spirit on the cross
called life. God accepts the offering and a slow transformation
is begun in us in ways we cannot comprehend. Like Christ we
live not for ourselves but for others. Humanity, done to death
by sin, is in a corpse-like condition. We raise it up from the
dead.

Because of our baptism we are the servant referred to in
today's readings. We are not so much Jesus-like as John-like
figures, precursors. In the mystery of faith we are, at the same
time, God's beloved offspring.

We are the covenant. In us the promise is made or broken.
Others experience in us their own covenant with God or they
do not. We are called to be light, to open the eyes of the blind
and bring prisoners out of darkness. It is we whom the LORD
calls upon for the victory of justice. We are "the covenant of
the people and the light of the nations" (Is 42:6).

I am not talking here about good example. If you live a
reasonably decent Christian life you are bound to give good
example. I am talking about the effects of baptism. St. Luke
describes what came with Jesus as not resembling a tame bath
in water but mighty wind and fire. Think of the high winds
you saw on television in Hawaii this fall, then later in
Louisiana. Think of the burning fuel tanks in Newark last
week. "We couldn't have stopped it," said the fire chief, "even
if we tried." But that is destructive wind and destructive fire,
you say. What kind of image is that for what happens in the
baptism of an infant child who has not even been consulted
about wishing to be a Christian? Listen to some imagery that
came to light with the discovery of Jewish papyrus scrolls

along the shores of the Dead Sea in the late 1940s. They come from the age that immediately preceded that of Jesus. John the Baptist, who — say the gospels — inhabited the same desert of Judea may have been nourished by this teaching.

[In the final age God will] purge by his truth all human deeds, refining [by fire] for himself some of humanity in order to remove every evil spirit from the midst of their flesh, to cleanse them with a holy Spirit from all wicked practices and sprinkle them with a spirit of truth like purifying water. (*Community Rule*, 1QS 4:20)

That is the imagery of cauterizing a wound, purging out dross in a smelting oven, cleansing soiled flesh with cooling water. It is what the gospels say was achieved in Jesus as he came on the public scene, to be prepared for his mission, God anointed him

with the Holy Spirit and power. He went about doing good works and healing all who were in the grip of the devil, and God was with him (Ac 10:38).

Why do we not proclaim the gospel? Why do we feel no compulsion to go on mission? It is a matter of conditioning, largely. Ours has become a clerical church in modern times —painfully so. If a thing issues from the bishop's office or the rectory we understand it. Otherwise, who can guess the response of a thin-skinned clergy to lay initiative? We have painted ourselves into a corner of passivity as a whole church. Besides, no Catholic who is not in holy orders has the say about spending a five-cent piece of contributed funds, not even a postage stamp. And while much in the line of evangelization costs nothing, it would be nice if zealous Catholics could forge ahead in a gospel project and tell their priests at the end of a fiscal period how they spent their own contributed money.

But we have the tradition of silent living of the gospel, we say. Every one of us knows someone at work or in the neighborhood who talks the ear off a brass monkey about all that Jesus has done for her, or the joys of being saved and how you too can be as happy as he is. The trouble is, the evangelical tradition of an endless flow of words has reduced those in the mainline churches to absolute silence about salvation. They literally have nothing to say. They cannot put into words how God saves the people of his love through the cross in the power of the spirit.

There is another dodge we have. We employ it when all else fails. We say: "It is not in the Catholic tradition to have had a personal, rememberable experience of Jesus Christ in our lives and the power of his saving love. We cannot name a day, an hour, when we accepted him as our personal savior. Rather, we cannot think of a time when he did *not* have that role in our lives." All quite true, I suppose. In fact, it is a recent innovation in Christian history, this "experimental religion" as they called it in the British Isles no earlier than the seventeenth century. We may be delighted that there is no test of emotion or exhilaration to validate our authentic belongingness as Christians. Still, there had to be a conversion experience at some point in our past — remembered or not — to ensure that the infant baptism in which sponsors spoke for us was not mere mummery, was not that Christian impossibility automatic religion.

At a certain point in the ancient baptismal rite there is an exorcism. In it the whole church prays that the demons of hell may lose all power over this adult or child. "Ephpheta," we say with Jesus in his native tongue. "Be thou opened!" We say it to each other today, we the mute witnesses to Christ who, out of embarrassment, fear, incapacity, lack of conviction, or whatever it may be, do not preach the gospel. "Be thou opened. Out of him, dumb spirit. Speak!" Evangelism is being so full of Christ you just cannot help sharing. God pity us if our emptiness is the cause of our silence. Maybe we do not want anyone to be as miserable, as inhibited, as victimized in our Catholic faith as we are. So be it. Don't say a word, in that case. But if you are so full of Christ you cannot help sharing, then for God's sake, *speak!*

January 9, 1983   St. James Church

EPIPHANY
Is 60:1-6; Eph 3:2-3, 5-6; Mt 2:1-12/Year B

"Rise up in splendor! Your light has come."

Today's feast of the Epiphany celebrates the fact that the power and wisdom of God have appeared in Jesus Christ.

In contrast to Christmas and to its Eastern predecessor the Epiphany — both of which have the incarnation or coming of the Redeemer as their subject — today's Western feast celebrates the manifestation of godhead in a man which continues over time. It is not a particular event that is being celebrated but a concept of faith, a concept that is visibly expressed in a whole series of events both in Jesus' miracles and the power of his words — and in *our* lives where God is no less powerful.

It would be discouraging indeed if God were visible and manifest only in someone long gone from us like Jesus. Lord and Christ he may be, but his presence at God's right hand would mean little if he was "God with us" only in memory and hope.

I have a poem stuck in a book somewhere, handwritten by a friend years ago, that I got out last night. The author is familiar enough, C. S. Lewis, but I have never seen the poem in print. It is about a bird's song, heard on Addison's Walk at Oxford early in the year — and English winters can be very cold. The bird said:

> This year time's nature will no more defeat you,
> Nor all the promised moments in their passing cheat you.
> This time they will not lead you round and back
> To autumn, one year older, by the well-worn track.

I should like to believe that this is so, but no bird ever sang that song to me. It takes more faith than I possess to say with the poet,

> This year, this year, as all these flowers foretell,
> We shall escape the circle and undo the spell.

If I am alive next Epiphany the shape of my existence should be much the same. Instead of escape from the rhythms of a predictable life, you and I have a life that is itself a rhythm. It is almost totally predictable. We call it life in a community of faith, a body. It is God's life in the midst of a people, and we are that people.

This means that the manifestation, the epiphany of God among us, is what can be seen and known on our faces and in our lives. There is as much of Jesus Christ, of God's holy Spirit abroad in the world as there is in us. Divine power is not confined to a book called the Bible, nor to the lives of saints and sages, nor to certain places on the earth like shrines and sanctuaries. It is everywhere or it is nowhere. It resides in us, God's creatures and his chosen ones, or there is no God.

Let us take the Christian case alone, though God is just as surely manifest in the Jew and Muslim who acknowledge him and in the myriad others who call him by every name and no name. In us we say that God exists personally but not individually, rather corporately, in Christ. Once this man was Jesus, an individual like the rest of us, but since his glorification he has become someone in whom we have our being. We say we are "in Christ." It is described as reciprocal in the fourth gospel: he is in us and we in him in mutual interpenetration. St. Paul does not use that vocabulary. We are in Christ, in his body, but it is the spirit — God's spirit which is the same as the spirit of Christ — that is in us. Jesus was born of Mary, a virgin, paid the normal price of mortality, but in being raised from the dead was the locus or place where believers in him and God came into one. The epiphany of God for all the ages will be that tatterdemalion army of saints and sinners we call the church.

On Sunday, by ancient designation *kyriakē*, the Lord's day, we assemble to let that Lord, that Christ, make us his body anew. We are forever in danger of slipping from our corporate existence in him back into individuality. The next step would be the nothingness from which we came. So we sit in pews and stand and kneel, we sing, at one point we tentatively embrace, and then we eat, to manifest to one another the Jesus Christ whom we are. We are not gods, God knows, but God is in us.

The chief signs that this is so are two: the proclaimed word, on which the homilist comments to aid reflection, and the bread broken and cup drunk. "Is not the cup of blessing we bless a sharing in the blood of Christ? Because the loaf is one we, many though we are, are one body, for we all partake in one loaf" (1 Cor 10:16-17).

I meet many people in the course of a week. So do you. They are associates at work and people pumping gas and at check-out counters and the weekly assortment of family members and friends. I know many of them very well but am close to a very few. There is however a shared intimacy with you — whose names in many cases I do not know — that is unique. Whether it be the 1:15 crowd or the congregation at 12:00 or 10:30 or 9:00 is not important. You are those in whose company God is made manifest to me weekly in a special way. I see his face in many places because I see him here — in his son Jesus Christ who corporately we are.

January 7, 1979   St. Stephen Martyr Parish

(The Sundays of the Year beginning with the Second, which follows the Feast of the Baptism of the Lord, are in Volume II, pp. 9 and following.)

LENT

FIRST SUNDAY OF LENT
Gn 2:7-9, 3:1-7; Rom 5:12-19; Mt 4:1-11/Year A

As we embark on Lent this morning — even though we are four days into it — we are faced with two stories and an allegory.

The allegory, the second reading, assigns a meaning to the first of the stories. It is a possible explanation but not the only one. Yet St. Paul's allegory about Christ has so prevailed that we tend to forget what the original tale is about. It is about the sin of self-sufficiency.

The first story from Genesis is simplicity itself. It has three characters. Literary people call this the rule of three: there once was an Englishman, a Scot and an Irishman; or a rabbi, a priest and a minister; in this case it is a man, a woman and a snake. The story is not a whimsy, though. It is told in deadly earnest. It explains how evil entered the world. At first all was orderly. A stream welled up out of the earth, watering the soil in every direction. You know about the parched deserts of the middle east from which the Bible came, so you can tell we are launched on a fantasy. Then the idyll is broken. Stark reality appears in the form of the clay of the earth and the breath of life. Together they make the human creature, *Adam* in Hebrew, made from the ruddy soil, *Adamah.*

He stands there in the midst of Eden, a paradise of pleasure.

Now all of this happened far to the east, which helps you to know how mysterious the whole thing was. The man is given a wife — he needs company, a partner in sex and marriage, and the beasts recently fashioned will not do. What makes the pair strangers in paradise is that tree. No, not the tree of life. Every other tale in the ancient world had a tree of life. It was the other tree, the one that gave knowledge of good and evil.

You can see that this is a pretty simple tale. Enter the snake. The snake for the ancient Semite was not so much wicked as cunning. It slithered through the grass and laid low the unwary. It shed its skin as it emerged from hibernation and moved on to a second career. The snake was a living parable of sexuality, with fire in its tip at the thrust. And it talked. Wily, clever talk, lying talk, setting the man against the woman and the woman against the man — and both, poor fools, against God. "He is envious of you, you know. He made you innocent, even a little dumb. But God is insecure. He doesn't know how long his superiority will last."

When the Greeks told this tale they had a chap named Prometheus who stole fire from the gods. The Jews' tale was of a pair that stole the mystery of life and the way to pass it on. They stole God's wisdom from God and it made a terrible difference. "Then the eyes of both were opened, and they realized they were naked." Have I said that this is a tale of sexuality and its use? Well, yes, at one level, it is. The interesting thing is, the part about shame has nothing to do with the part about sex. Nakedness to the Semite meant humiliation, being brought low. If you were despoiled of the clothes which preserved you in dignity, nakedness made you a laughing-stock.

It is the simplest of tales. It is the profoundest of tales. It is about basic human arrogance, the sin of self-sufficiency. Humanity is told to trust. It refuses to trust and pays the price. Indeed, it *does* know good from evil and wishes to God it didn't.

The second tale is just as simple as the first. This time the characters are two but the setting, which is threefold, makes a third: the desert, the parapet of the temple, the high mountain. Without these, the tale could not be told. Jesus' adversary is named simply that: *diábolos*, in Greek, "adversary."

He is more. He is "the tester" (Mt 4:3). Of old there was a talking serpent. Now you have a talking angel. But in both cases a tempter. The gospel tale does not go as far back as human origins but only to Israel's origins as a liberated people, sorely tempted as it was on the Sinai. Would they have enough to eat, they wondered, would they make it through to Canaan, would they continue to worship the one God? They failed all three tests miserably — sustenance, safety, power. Their God offered all three benefits to them and they refused. But where Israel, God's daughters and sons, would not trust, Jesus, God's son, did trust. The power of Jesus' obedience is stronger than the power of the devil's rebellion. He is the true *Adam*, image of God (Heb 1:3). He is the source of life, the source of good (Jn 17:1-2).

Lent is upon us, making its demands. They are not the demands of self-control for we are not Stoic philosophers. We are followers of Christ, the baptized. That means that in him we obey God and can be strong. We do not trust in our own powers, to succumb thereby in weakness. We are human, sprung from the first Adam who trusted in himself. Death reigns in us because of sin. The gift of the second man, Jesus Christ, is overflowing grace and righteousness. In him we can live. We need not die.

A single offense brought condemnation to all, but a single righteous act brought all acquittal and life. It is the business of Lent, quite simply, to help us know that, to bring home to us that our true strength lies in our obedience like that of Jesus, not a trust in self alone like that of Adam.

Whatever our sin, it comes down to a lack of trust in the One who sustains us. Is cynicism our sin? Is it sex with someone not ours in marriage? Psychic support from more drink than we need? Deriving that lift from the instant superiority which bad-mouthing others affords? In every case it is a lack of trust, a turning to the creature as our savior. We make a settlement with our need that is of our own devising.

We seek an integration of our unfulfilled selves, an end to the alienation of our being that goes much deeper. It can be in other areas entirely like household tyranny or making peers at work look bad to heighten our small authority, our greater skill. All sin is a dull business. It does not require zooming up to the parapet of the temple or seeing all the kingdoms of the world. An overview of our tiny little world will do.

Lent is healing time, coming to our senses time, acknowledging where our happiness lies time. It is a season to help us trust in God and not ourselves — which is the whole meaning of our redemption.

March 8, 1981   St. Paul's Parish

FIRST SUNDAY IN LENT
Gn 9:8-15; 1 Pt 3:18-22; Mk 1:12-15/Year B

Lent began on Wednesday with the rite of ashes. There are many who were with us on that day who are not here today. Again, perhaps many more are here at Sunday worship than could gather for that rite. In any case, a church centered on the Lord's Day thinks of today as the beginning of Lent, a season that has as its primary history the final preparation of adult catechumens for full lives as Christians.

There are a few such in this congregation. The greater number by far are the long-baptized. We join our prospective new members in Christ (or in this Catholic communion) in the study of the Bible, prayer, and fasting both to give them heart and to acquire for ourselves a renewed sense of Christian purpose. With Easter night the season's purpose will be

accomplished — if we let it do for us all that it can in the
midst of a praying church.

Are you isolated at times in the midst of a family, desolate
because you feel cut off from all human companionship,
alienated from those who ought to be your friends and peers? I
do not think of this congregation as a body of misfits but as a
perfectly normal spread of human types. That is why, as your
preacher, I feel free to confess my own isolation at times,
suspecting it is the case of everyone here. In such a season of
suffering I am not comforted. God seems far away, my
existence pointless; my sense that everyone is against me or
totally disinterested in me is at its highest point. This is not my
normal state but when it overtakes me it is real. I assume the
same is true for you at times; for some of you, for long
stretches of time.

Jesus knew the human reality of which I speak. Mark
reports it simply, almost as if he has no interest in the human
feelings of Jesus. In doing this he is in the great story-telling
tradition, engaging the reader deeply with a few swift strokes.

Who is this "son of God" (1:1) that the Spirit can *drive* him
into the desert? (That phrase was too much for Matthew, who
in 4:1 softened it to say that "Jesus was *led* by the Spirit.")
Who is Satan that he is free to "put him to the test"? And how
can jackals and desert cats discomfit a person who has the
angels of God to comfort him?

The drama is a set piece, of course. Long familiarity with
the Bible in Greek would have cast light on each phrase for
Mark's hearers. It can do the same for us. This is the story of a
just man troubled by the "Satan" of the tale of Job (Job 1:6-12;
see Zech 3:1-2 and 1 Chr 21:1). The just man Jesus is sent off
to the desert. The place was home to nomads but a real threat

to grazing and agricultural Israel. Messengers of God attend this Jesus who, for Mark and for us, is God's emissary sent to inaugurate the last age. John the Baptist is deftly removed from the scene to give place to Jesus in Galilee — the first and last place of the gospel's proclamation in the narrative of Mark (1:14; 14:28; 16:7).

Mark, the first gospel to be written, is completely absorbed with the idea of discipleship. As things were for Jesus, so they must be for his followers. If he, after the pattern of John, proclaimed the good news of God, so must those who come after him. This ringing call of Jesus announces that the rule of God over human lives is nigh. Turn clear around in your tracks, it says. Become believers in the only gospel that Jesus — and Mark his disciple after him — ever announced. Use Lent as a desert time, a time of testing to prepare yourselves to be about life's business of proclaiming the gospel.

Do I need to ask you to simulate a scene of personal desolation? Chances are that is unnecessary. The severe weather is a great help in this season, whether for the house-bound or those who must get around in it. Even the fully active and those most favored by climate experience the long stretch between Christmas and Easter. It is a time of routine and sameness, a desert of the dullness of our lives. Is the time redeemable? The church has thought so, ever since it initiated the lenten time of preparation for our anticipated rising with Christ our passover. To be of the church is to ransom this oppressive time, in which hope is kept alive as the days lengthen. ("Lent" comes from the word "lengthen.") Our power to endure late winter comes from the Easter hope symbolized by the sun climbing in the heavens. As the days grow longer so does our hope.

Genesis tells a different tale than Mark today, the very opposite of desert existence. It is a story of raging waters that prove saving waters for Noah and his family. The first epistle of Peter makes the most of that story. We are the ones, now not a few like the eight of Noah's day, but the many who in the ark of the church ride the flood of baptism. Water has not been a sign of destruction for us but of salvation. It is a sure pledge of God that we can be irreproachable in conscience if we give water's symbolism power through faith in Christ risen.

We a people of irreproachable conscience, sinful and confused as we are? Is the biblical author dreaming? Yet this is the lenten possibility and the Easter hope. We can emerge from six weeks in the desert a purified people, ready to proclaim the gospel anew with clean lips like those of Jesus the son of God.

Our Lutheran companions in faith do better than the rest of us, perhaps, in choosing as the second reading today that stirring passage with which Paul concludes Romans 8:

If God is for us, who can be against us? . . . Who shall bring a charge against God's chosen ones? God, who justifies? Who shall condemn them? Christ Jesus, who died or rather was raised up, who is at the right hand of God and who intercedes for us? Who will separate us from the love of Christ? Trial, or distress, or persecution, or hunger, or nakedness, or danger, or the sword? As Scripture says: "For your sake we are being slain all the day long; we are looked upon as sheep to be slaughtered." Yet in all this we are more than conquerors because of him who has loved us. For I am certain that neither death nor life, neither angels nor principalities, neither the present nor the future, nor powers, neither height nor depth nor any other creature, will be able to separate us from the love of God that comes to us in Christ Jesus, our Lord.

Those who chose this passage know the intimacy of the life of faith at its highest and best. They know who is for us as our savior to help us identify whatever might be against us: loneliness, oppression because of our sex or the way the mystery of sex affects us, the pain of growing up, the regrets and pains of advancing age.

As followers of Jesus we are in some sense invincible — not with the triumph of a sloganeering sect, not with the smug satisfaction that "all others will be damned," but with the gospel conviction that the God who is mighty has done great things for us. God has done these things for us in Christ, if only we will submit ourselves to the purifying test.

February 28, 1982   St. Paul's Parish

FIRST SUNDAY OF LENT
Dt 26:4-10; Rom 10:8-13; Lk 4:1-13/Year C

If you stand on the ruins of ancient Jericho — sometimes called "the oldest city in the world" — on the outskirts of modern Jericho and look due west back in the direction of the Jerusalem road, you see a rugged cliff face which the locals call, in Arabic, *Jebel Qarantal*. It means the "forty-day mountain." This is the site of a monastery going back to the third century whose later ruins still stand. Early Christian piety had to locate everything described in the gospels, even when the evangelists did not provide sufficient clues. The temptation narrative in today's gospel is completely elusive geographically speaking. It describes a series of three visions — not in the historical order but in the realm of prophetic fulfillment. Israel in its wanderings on the Sinai peninsula was tempted sorely, and in three ways: over food — that is, having enough to eat; over idolatry — believing in the LORD or the gods of the peoples they encountered; and over basic trust — would their God see them through safely or not? An early Christian hand took what is a brief statement in Mark that Jesus was tested in the desert by Satan for forty days (1:13) and worked it up into a scenario that Matthew and Luke both drew on. In Luke's contrast between Jesus and his people of old, Jesus succeeded in the tests where they had failed. The man of Nazareth quoted from Deuteronomy twice in response to Satan's attempts to make him doubt God's power. A third time, "the devil quoted Scripture to his own purpose," as the proverb has it. Jesus came back at Satan's misuse of two verses from a psalm (91:12) by saying: "You shall not put the LORD your God to the test" (Dt 6:16).

It is clear why we use this passage from Luke as today's gospel reading. Lent probably began on this Sunday before they added the first four days to make it a season of forty weekdays. It got its start as the final preparation time for the new adult candidates for baptism; their last weeks were a series of testings, even as their whole post-baptism life would be a life of challenge. In gospel times Jesus prevailed over humanity's ancient enemy, the devil. Would these converts-to-be — exorcised of Satan's baleful power in a series of "scrutinies" as they were called — likewise stand fast? The spirit of the Bible readings on all the lenten Sundays is one of readying for a test, entry into a new state, professing a faith publicly. Watch for it as we proceed from week to week.

It would be so much easier to understand Lent if we were a small, cohesive community witnessing the entry into our midst of certain adults, certain families, whom we all knew. There is a Benedictine monk from Newton Abbey in Sussex County with whom I studied briefly in the seminary and with whom I resumed friendship lately after a forty-year lapse. Along the way he spent 15 years in Tanzania; his is a missionary congregation. The pastor whom he now assists told me this winter of Fr. Kevin's delight a year ago at preparing some people for reception into the church. The pastor asked in amazement, "Didn't you do that all the time in Africa?" "Never," he said. "The people had all been Catholics four, five and six generations. We never had any converts."

It came to be that way in Europe after the year 1000. By then, everybody was a Catholic of some degree. All the christenings were done in infancy. And with that develop-ment the whole focus of Lent changed. It shifted away from the conversion and faith of new believers and became a church-wide attempt to recapture the fervor of early youth. Penitential practices like fasting were adopted, there was almsgiving, and attempts were made at expanded preaching of the Bible to non-literate congregations. Alas, it was not easy to recall what Lent had been about! For the very people around whom all the activity had centered — the new believers repentant over their past sins and eager to learn and to do —were missing.

That is roughly our condition in a new parish that is not yet employing the Rite for the Christian Initiation of Adults. You read of it, perhaps, in the neighboring Trenton Diocese and elsewhere. It is a post-Vatican II restoration of ancient practice which carried people along in instruction in Catholic living —over a year or more — until just before Lent. Then they are inscribed as catechumens and the last six weeks of intense preparation begin. We have to have these people in mind wherever they are, all through Lent: the never yet baptized; Catholics in name only who wish to become so in fact; people of other Christian backgrounds whose Catholicity may be their first serious religious commitment. They do not proliferate in our midst for a number of reasons: one is, we are intensely private about our religion; again, we may not be convinced that being Catholics would bring them joy so why trouble them? Most tragic of all, there is no genuine Catholic community to invite them to. The symbol of all this is the infrequency with which the faith in our hearts becomes confession on our lips.

Paul writes to the Romans as if nothing else but this evangelization can constantly be going on. The word is near to us, he says, near to all of us. One need not scale the heavens to find it or cross the distant sea. It is as close to us as our very hearts or can be. The way to discover whether that is so is to confess it with our lips. "Jesus is Lord" is the simplest and probably the earliest Catholic creed. If we believe that "Jesus is Lord," our basic baptismal creed, then we will want to proclaim it, share it with all the world. It is no empty phrase, no mindless sloganeering. It is a truth filled with consequences. If Jesus is Lord, there is no aspect of our lives, no portion of our day that escapes his lordship.

Jesus is no Big Brother as in George Orwell's novel *1984*, a cosmic spy on all we do; he is not a shouting evangelical who expects us to rattle on in his praise twenty-four hours a day. Jesus is the love that bonds us together, the mutual respect that allows us to despise no one especially society's least members, the reason why unconcern for peace or justice for all is not allowed us. To say "Jesus is Lord" and mean it is to begin to live life differently; to know that letting vicious, anti-human settlements continue is all wrong for the believer who may not sanction them for a moment.

Jew and Greek was the great social and religious split in Paul's day; they are no different, he said, to one who has faith in the Lord. There was no Jewish advantage over the gentile. For us it is black and white, surely. The great block of Afro-Americans, 11% of our nation, largely Christian though after three hundred years here God knows why, are the ones we have victimized, kept down, deprived of decent education, decent housing, decent jobs, and for whom we have created the euphemistic title "the functionally unemployed." With our lips we proclaim "Jesus is Lord." With our every political and social act we deny that he is Lord of all. "Everyone who calls on the name of the Lord will be saved," says Paul quoting the prophet Joel (3:5). You need clean lips for that, clean hands, a clean heart.

"My father was a wandering Aramean who went down to Egypt with a small household and lived there as an alien (Dt 26:5). . . . When the Egyptians maltreated and oppressed us . . . we cried to the. . . God of our father, and he heard our cry and saw our affliction. . . . He brought us into this country, this land flowing with milk and honey." Being a Catholic, like being a Jew, is not to live in an earthly paradise. But it is knowing who and what you are as a member of the baptized, a person sealed with the Spirit. God's mark is on our forehead like a brand. We are forever, irrevocably, irreversibly his own. It is a blessed fate, not an indifferent or a tragic one. We are God's people, the sheep of his flock.

We have a six-week opportunity to reflect on the glory of being Christian in a worldwide communion — and to share the word with anyone who will give us a hearing.

February 20, 1983   St. James Church

SECOND SUNDAY OF LENT
Gn 12:1-4; 1 Tm 1:8-10; Mt 17:1-9/Year A

The first eleven chapters of Genesis are meant as a kind of pre-history, describing those far-off, improbable days to a Jew before there were any Jews. The real story of Israel starts today in Chapter 12 with the call of a man from Ur named Abram. The Bible places Ur in Chaldea, modern Iraq. Haran, where the family settled for a time on its journey westward over the fertile crescent, is in modern Turkey. And Canaan, through which they passed on the way to the Negev, the southern desert, is of course Israel and the annexed west bank and Jordan. I saw a clip on last night's news of the kibbutz where Moshe Dayan was a young man — in connection with the likelihood that he will form a new party and run for prime minister. In the few minutes the countryside was visible on the screen, the great beauty of the land came home to me once again. The poor Canaanites! How could they have guessed that Abram's wandering caravan spelled an end to them? You did not see any Canaanites on TV last night, no Perizzites, no people of Shinar or Elam, no Rephaim or Zuzim, no Horites or Amalekites or Amorites. Only Jews and Egyptians. But the Eygptians you saw were not the Egyptians of the Bible except for an occasional Copt in the crowd.

It is a great mystery, this perseverance of the Jews as a people over centuries. The eyes of faith see the key to it in the promise that provides our first reading:

I will make of you a great nation,
    and I will bless you;
I will make your name great,
    so that you will be a blessing. . . .

All the communities of the earth
  shall find blessing in you.

The LORD's blessing means a sharing and an increase of life. It means fertility and prosperity, rest and refreshment, posterity and peace. The awful trend of the first eleven chapters is reversed: ejection from paradise, fratricide, flood; the witless slaughter of Lamech, the confusion of tongues and dispersal of nations at Babel. The LORD has taken the initiative to reverse the spread of evil and Abraham — as he will come to be — has responded with the obedience of faith.

Years later the Christian author we call Luke would write:

He has dealt mercifully with our fathers,
  and remembered the holy covenant he made,
The oath he swore to Abraham our father he would grant us:
  that, rid of fear and delivered from the enemy,
We should serve him devoutly through all our days
  and be holy in his sight (1:72-75)

If you live a faithful life that canticle of Zechariah will be spoken over you as you are lowered into the earth — a hymn to a faithful God who keeps his promise to and through the Jews.

"God has saved us and called us to a holy life," our lenten instruction continues, "not because of any merit of ours but according to . . . the grace held out to us in Christ Jesus before the world began, but now made manifest through the appearance of our Savior. He has robbed death of its power and has brought life and immortality into clear light through the gospel" (2 Tm 1:9-10). The promise spoken to Abraham continues in force: grace has preceded evil; life will not be conquered by death.

I met a man at breakfast this week, an older man wearing his son's college ring which, it turned out upon inquiry, was from the University of California. The son had been killed in the Tet offensive — late January of 1968. I was bleary-eyed at breakfast on Thursday, having stayed up very late reading a book about the U.S. intelligence community. It was *The Man Who Kept the Secrets* (Richard Helms) by Thomas Powers. The book told in detail how the Johnson White House desperately wanted North Vietnamese troop strength to be around 300,000 — Rostow, Bundy, McNamara, the whole team except George Ball. A young CIA analyst, a man I happen to know from Waterford, Virginia, had gone through a mountain of paper in Langley and concluded that there were at least 600,000 Viet Cong under arms. He had flown to Saigon with two others to convince the military the previous autumn that "our basic problem is that we've been told to keep the numbers under 300,000." I could only tell Mr. Bavoretto at breakfast that I was sorry he had lost his son.

That isn't all I read this week. There was a copy of *Mademoiselle* within my reach — a magazine the subscription to which I have let lapse — and I read through an article telling me which contraceptive was the best for me to reduce my fears — so I wouldn't feel "I was making love on a trampoline or a slippery deck," and so on. Fear of side effects can have a depressing effect on the whole proceedings. "And after all, that's what choosing a congenial sex partner and the device that's right for you is all about, isn't it — the maximum pleasure with the minimum of anxiety?" I am quoting from memory but think I have it pretty straight.

Some weeks it is not so easy to concentrate on the mystery of our salvation, even some weeks in Lent.

We were created for life and the love of God, more powerful than our weakness, has conquered death (see Rom 8:28-30; Heb 2:14). I believe that. I try to live as if it were so, as if the epistle to the Romans and a writing like Hebrews had life straight. But when you run into the death and pleasure industries going full tilt, you sometimes wonder. It is not that God has not been faithful to his promise. It is that we get too busy living for ourselves to care whether God promised anything or not.

The transfiguration gospel appears in the lenten liturgy for roughtly the same reasons it was written in the first place. The believers of Matthew's time, like Mark's before him, had every reason to wonder if the risen life that was their hope would ever come to pass for them. They were given a tale of anticipated glory in the life of Jesus who had to suffer and die. Similarly, the catechumens of later centuries, with their baptism only four or five weeks off, began to get cold feet at the prospect of their new life. A clean break with lying, gossip, overindulgence in eating and drinking, sexual adventures. It was not exactly "cold turkey." They had been living by this code for a couple of years. But "*never* again"? And so they are given the vision of glory at the top of the mountain before they are asked to "bear the hardships which the gospel entails" (2 Tm 1:8). They fall to the ground, overcome with fear. Jesus breaks the spell. "Get up. Do not be afraid."

Get up and get living. This life of holiness is real.

Have you had a good dose of the cross? Or are you young and has it not touched you yet? Older, and do you wonder why not? Don't worry. We are doing this thing together: carrying about in our bodies his dying so that in our bodies the *life* of Jesus may also be relived.

March 15, 1981   St. David the King Church

SECOND SUNDAY OF LENT
Gn 22:1-2, 9, 10-13, 15-18; Rom 8:31-34; Mk 9:1-9/Year B

We are just ten days into the lenten season and are reminded early in it by today's gospel of where the journey will take us. That surely is the meaning of Mark's transfiguration narrative, which two of the other evangelists will pick up. Jesus has told Peter after his confession of faith in him, "You are the Christ", that the "Son of man must suffer many things and be rejected...and be killed, and after three days rise again" (8:29ff.). The careful structure of Mark — our gospel for this year — establishes that Jesus' glory was hard bought. He has conquered death but not without first being conquered by death. To his disciples he proposes the same. "If anyone would come after me, let that one deny very selfhood and take up the cross to follow me.... For what does it profit anyone to gain the whole world and forfeit life itself?" (vv. 34, 36). And so the story proceeds — establishing carefully what human life is and what is its worth. "There are some standing here" — Mark's contemporaries — "who will not taste death before they see the rule of God come with power."

I say the same to you. If you live lives of fidelity and discipleship you will see marvels of conversion, generosity, service, submission to God's inscrutable will that you would not think possible. For it is not only the Lord who is transfigured. It is we ourselves who like him are called to be Easter people. God can, God will effect the change in us. Be patient in faith. Let it happen to you.

What were the thoughts of the favored three Peter, James, and John as they trudged up the high mountain with their tireless, wordless friend? That they would fail him on another mountain their eyes heavy with sleep (14:40); that all would forsake him and flee (v. 50)? I doubt it. Mark the narrator knew that. The spineless trio — young men in search of power and influence — could not have had a clue. They *may* have thought of the best-known tale of a wordless mountain climb in the history of their people. The hill was called Moriah, "Lookout Mountain" in English. We cannot place it, though later tradition made it the temple mount in Jerusalem. On it is that handsome basalt formation housed by the mosque called the Dome of the Rock. Jewish piety made it the slab on which Abraham stood ready to sacrifice his son. "And Abraham took the wood of the burnt offering and laid it on Isaac his son; and he took in his hand the fire and the knife."

I say the three disciples may have thought of that tale but I do not know that. I only know that the legend of the binding of Isaac was very much to the fore in first-century Jewish thinking. It probably supplied Paul with the rabbinic paradigm for his theory of Jesus' expiatory sacrifice. But Peter, James, and John — as our story opens — are still thinking thoughts of fame and fortune. Jesus' somber silence could have triggered remembrance in them, however. "Here are the fire and the wood; but where is the lamb for the offering?" Poor innocent boy, knowing nothing of the terrible things God asks of people. But Abraham knew. And Jesus that young old man knew. No wonder both were silent trudging up the hill. "And he took the wood of the . . . offering and laid it on his son."

Søren Kierkegaard in "Fear and Trembling" has a marvelous meditation on the Genesis story. He says the boy must have cried out to his father as the knife was upraised: "Don't do it! You're ruining everything." Why then *did* he do it? For God's sake and, in complete identity with this, for his own sake. God wanted proof of his faith and Abraham wanted to give such proof. The two points of view came together in a test, a temptation. Ordinarily, people are tempted by what would keep them from doing their duty. Here the temptation consists in doing the right thing, the ethical thing, sparing your boy. Faith goes a step beyond the ethical, says Kierkegaard. "Abraham gives up the finite to grasp the infinite, and in doing so he appalls me." Suppose he is mistaken. What can save him? He renounces everything: the son he loves, the possibility of progeny. He suspends the ethical entirely to lay hold of the sublime joy of faith. "Faith is a miracle," says Kierkegaard, "yet no one is excluded from it; for that in which all human life is unified is passion, and faith is a passion."

I received a letter last week from a friend of many years, a woman who writes that she will be settled in at Siuna in godforsaken northeast Nicaragua by now. She used to be the chairman of the theology department at an eastern Catholic college, a colleague there (not Georgetown) of Jeanne Kirkpatrick, who has quite different ideas about what to do about Nicaragua. I could have grown depressed about the quality of my friend's faith and my lack of it.

Kierkegaard was of great help here. He paints a picture of what he calls a "knight of faith," a man who has opted to live at the border of finitude and infinity.

> He tends to his work. To look at him you might think he had the soul of a bookkeeper, so precise is he. He takes Sunday off; goes to church. He looks like everybody else in the congregation. No heavenly glance or any other token of the incommensurable betrays him. His vigorous hymn-singing proves at the most that he has a good chest. He lives as carefree as a ne'er-do-well, and yet he buys up the acceptable time at the dearest price, for he does not do the least thing except by virtue of the absurd.

There is my Sister friend, off with her new friends, surrounded by the transplanted Miskito Indians. There is Jesus on his high mountain, overshadowed by a cloud, hearing a voice calling him "my beloved son." And here are we, not in working-class Copenhagen but in bourgeois Somerset County, trying to do nothing — God helping us — but live by faith, by virtue of the absurd.

March 7, 1982   St. James Church

SECOND SUNDAY OF LENT
Gn 15:5-12, 17-18; Phil 3:17—4:1; Lk 9:28b-36/Year C

The Jews call Abraham their Father because they spring from him. The Muslims who venerate him equally call him "the Friend" — friend to God and because of his defense of his nephew Lot and his hospitality to the three visitors at Mamre, friend to man. We Christians call him our Father in faith because of his trust in God, which God credited to him as righteousness. What would the Canaanites and Perizzites call him if they were alive today? Probably "imperialist," "colonialist," and "thief."

It gives an American a funny feeling to stand before the monument to the Mexican dead in Chapultepec Park in Mexico City, and read there the sins of our fathers in the Mexican War who stole a land from a people. Abraham did something like that when he migrated west from Mesopotamia, first all the way down to Egypt, then up through the desert to Hebron and the land of Canaan. In modern Hebron is his burial place near that of Rebecca, Isaac, and Jacob — for long centuries a mosque but now in Jewish hands.

I read lately of an inner-city junior high school where the February bulletin board carried pictures of Washington, Jefferson, and Jackson. Underneath was written, in sequence, "Slave-owner," "Emancipator?" and "Indian-killer." A lot depends on who writes the history books. The only Abraham who has come down to us looks like an authentic hero, given the bloody code of conduct of those times. The pattern of migration forces him out of Chaldea, down near where Tigris and Euphrates run together. He then comes to Haran and after that goes southward with his flocks and herds. Famine is what drives him chiefly, says the Bible, although centuries later when he has become a folk-hero his movements are interpreted as a series of calls from God.

We in this country should recognize him readily, steeped in the frontier tradition as we are from years of movie westerns. Abraham sets out for the unknown full of trust in his God, convinced that somewhere out there was a land he could someday call his own. Like our own pilgrims and explorers, when Abraham got to that land he found that to call it his own he would have to steal it from the people who had got there first. When you read in Genesis 14 how Abram the Hebrew leagued with the king of Sodom and his allies to whip Chedorlaomer of Elam and the three kings he looks heroic. "Give me the people; the goods you may keep," says the king of Sodom after their victory. Abram piously refuses: "I have sworn to the Lord . . . that I will not take so much as thread or a sandal-strap . . . lest you should say, 'I made Abram rich.'" It would ill-befit us to doubt the story but the Israelites wrote it. The account of the defeated Elamites does not remain. One

can only think of the liberated plains Indians, the liberated
Cubans, Filipinos, Virgin Islanders, Samoans. We set them all
free but some were so ignorant that they had to do it over
again for themselves.

But it will not do to fault the history-writing of the Bible.
We should be grateful that in Abraham we have an authentic
hero, a thoroughly decent man. He conducts himself well
every time we meet him. In today's liturgy we meet him doing
a strange thing but one that is terribly important to us.
Abraham is "cutting" a covenant. A bargain is struck, God's
word is given. The land and children will be Abraham's. As a
sign of this bargain three animals and two birds are hacked
apart. The sun goes down, vultures are fought off and Abraham falls into a trance. Then a flaming torch passes between
the parts of the animals in the terrifying darkness. The
symbolism of the bloody separation was, "If either of us
defaults on this promise, so may it happen to us." The unseen
God cut apart like a heifer or a ram? Well, not really. But the
seriousness of the event is compared to that between a
powerful king and weaker one where the former sets the
terms, all of them favorable to the lesser recipient. This is the
notion of covenant. It is a notion that is with us still, right up
to today's celebration of Mass.

We celebrate a renewed covenant that is an everlasting one.
The symbol this time is not blood and fire and smoke. It is not
even the mangled body of a man on a cross though that is the
appearance given. The symbol of God's faithfulness to us in
the new covenant is a totally obedient man, Jesus: a faithful
man, a man who will never go back on his word as God does
not go back on his. There is no one we know of quite like this.
That is the uniqueness of Jesus. It is not his blood that is

important; the blood is only a result, an outcome. The greatness of Jesus is his faithfulness, the cause of the bloodshed.

The other two readings fit in readily enough. Jesus converses with Moses and Elijah, the two great covenant figures besides Abraham. He is visibly transfigured before Peter, James, and John. The reading from Philippians says we too will be *if we stay faithful to the terms of the covenant.*

What is the fidelity that brings as its result eternal life? We used to say things like not missing Mass and observing the feasts and keeping the lenten fast; but they are external things like the blood on calvary. They are not what matters. God sees the inner spirit. God sees the heart.

If we are to keep our part of the covenant which has Christ's body and blood as its signs we must abhor all bloodshed. That, after all, is why he died at the hands of senseless men: to bring an end to blind hate that thinks it can solve anything by destroying human life.

Do we keep our part of the covenant? We do not. We support wars without a murmur. We let our sons be turned into killers and wonder why they go berserk when they come home. We let an army machine divide the country into a black and white of hatred, turning to interracial education in the military for the first time last week because we cannot get them to hate and kill the enemy, they are so busy fighting each other. We hail Corporal Calley everywhere he goes in Georgia — our hero, our little killing machine. "It was no big deal, sir."

No, we do not keep our part of the covenant. We love blood. We love the spirit that destroyed Jesus. And it is destroying us.

The call to covenant-renewal, to lenten existence is clean contrary to the national spirit of war-making and racism. Let us not only repent. Let us know how alienated we Christians are called to be from the life, the mood, the spirit of our own American people, our kinsfolk (as Paul said) for whom there is great grief and constant pain in our hearts.

March 7, 1971   Our Lady of Mercy Parish

THIRD SUNDAY OF LENT
Ex 17:3-7; Rom 5:1-2, 5-8; Jn 4:5-42/Year A

"It is precisely in this that God proves his love for us: that while we were still sinners, Christ died for us" (Rom 5:8). While we were still sinners! That is not some distant age far away and long ago — back in Moses' day, in Jesus' day. That was last week, last night: all the bitter infighting at work, the cruel recriminations of spouses and best friends, the people young and old who fell asleep quite senseless from dope or drink at 3:00 this morning. Sins of weakness, sins of power, sins of pride. Yet it is certain we shall be saved by Christ from God's wrath if we have faith. Christ, the holy one, died for us in our godlessness. That is an archaic word, "godlessness," meaning something very familiar like stubbornness, pettiness, mean-spiritedness, all three — the determined will to live our lives without God, leaving a very human self in command. But, says St. Paul, it is still possible to realize our hope, because the love of God has been poured out in our hearts through the

Holy Spirit who has been given to us. His love is like a river, a cooling stream amidst a desert of selfishness.

That is the message of Lent: that although life is dull and wintry and drab, although sin is as real as any reality we know, there is hope.

The biblical figure for that hope is water. During the Exodus, at Rephidim deep down on the Sinai peninsula, there was no water. The people grumble — the place names "Massah" and "Meribah" mean "the testing" and "the quarreling" respectively. "What shall I do with these people?" says the despairing Moses. "A little more and they will stone me." This is where John's gospel gets its threat by the Jerusalem crowds at the end of Chapter 8 to stone Jesus. He is portrayed as a prophet-Moses figure throughout that gospel. No hardship that Moses endured can Jesus escape.

He is that very same Moses-figure at Jacob's well in the hostile territory of Samaria. "Sir," said the woman, "I can see you are a prophet." He is at least that for us Christians. We might even say, he is above all that. He is a teacher or spokesman for God, someone we can trust completely — about sin, about death, about the conduct of our life this next week.

The problem in John's gospel this morning is one of water rights, just as in an old western on late-night television. The well of the patriarch Jacob, who gave his nephew his new name "Israel" ("contender with God," Gn 32:29) to the Jewish people, is in Jesus' day in the hands of those kinfolk they have declared non-Jews. That was a stunning humiliation, and the rivalry with Samaria was intense. To a member of this hated people, a woman even, Jesus promises not Jacob's well but a well that will never run dry. Like Moses of old he

strikes the rock of Samaritan hearts and Jewish hearts —name
your people and you have named sinners — "and the water
will flow from it for the people to drink" (Ex 17:6).

Today's readings have a long history as the Scriptures
proclaimed on the mid-lenten Sunday. They hold out a
promise, the promise of water and new life for the adults
craving baptism who have only four weeks to go.

> Whoever drinks the water I give
>> will never be thirsty;
> no, the water I give
>> shall become a fountain within,
> leaping up into eternal life (v. 14).

They hold out the promise to *us*, the long-baptized, of finally
living the life we were committed to in infancy. I mean living it
now, which is what Jesus meant. Jesus being a good Jew was
not much for heaven or the after-life, though being in the
Pharisee tradition he was committed to the resurrection of the
dead. The development of a bodiless life in bliss came later. His
"eternal life" was the life of the final age of earth — here, now.
Jesus told a story in Luke's gospel of a poor beggar comforted
in Abraham's bosom. Matthew describes Jesus as saying at the
judgment to those who fed and clothed and visited others,
"Come, you blessed of my Father." But the "eternal life" of
John's gospel is a present reality, even though it has future
reference. It is the life of the baptized, a fountain, a torrent
within: their parched lives are slaked by the cooling waters of
grace, a God who loves.

Is Jesus, then, in John 4 with the Samaritan woman as in
John 3 with Nicodemus, speaking of the re-birth of "born
again Christians," a much later breed? He is, to be sure, in the

ancient catholic sense, the ancient orthodox sense. Faith in Christ has always meant new life for the Christian. Faith, a personal relation with God, made manifest by the symbol of a bath in water is new life, it is being born again, or it is nothing. The water-baptized Catholic or Orthodox or Protestant of infancy may have an adult or an adolescent conversion. Many do. During courtship, when a first child comes, in war, at the time of religious profession, at any crisis time in conscious life. Most Christians ratify the sacrament of infancy by conscious choice at some time although, tragically, perhaps some never do. Hence, to *know* that you are reborn, to will it, choose it, embrace it, is a possibility for the Christian at any time. It could happen this Lent for the first time to you. There is a born-again Christian, however, of whom the New Testament knows nothing. It is the person who, once "saved," can never be condemned; who looks on fellow Christians and fellow humans with a superiority that is contempt disguised as concern: poor creatures, they have not been "saved." They may be Lutherans or Presbyterians or Catholics but they are not "Christians" because they have not been born again, on our terms, on our narrow and exclusive reading — misreading, actually — of the holy Scriptures which with a marvelous docility turn out to say exactly what we want them to say.

May I read you a poem? I don't do this to you often, although I'd like to. Poetry is not everyone's favorite form of hearing the gospel preached. This is a sonnet that has no name, only that of its first line. It was written in the last century by an Englishman named Gerard Hopkins. There are a couple of unusual words in it: "brake" meaning a thicket and "chervil," a green used in soups, like carrot or collard greens. The whole poem has the Christian addressing God in complaint:

Thou art indeed just, Lord, if I contend
With thee; but, sir, so what I plead is just.
Why do sinners' ways prosper? and why must
Disappointment all I endeavour end?
Wert thou my enemy, O thou my friend,
How wouldst thou worse, I wonder, than thou dost
Defeat, thwart me? Oh, the sots and thralls of lust
Do in spare hours more thrive than I that spend,
Sir, life upon thy cause. See, banks and brakes
Now, leaved how thick! laced they are again
With fretty chervil, look, and fresh wind shakes
Them; birds build — but not I build; no, but strain,
Time's eunuch, and not breed one work that wakes.
Mine, O thou lord of life send my roots rain.

(Justus Quidem Tu es, Domine)

That is the cry of a born-again believer in mid-Lent, dry,
parched, calling out for the relief that Easter affords.

March 22, 1981   St. Paul's Parish

THIRD SUNDAY OF LENT
Ex 20:1-17; 1 Cor 1:22-25; Jn 2:13-25/Year B

Moses, you will recall, smashed the stone tablets on which
the ten commandments were written when he came down
from Mt. Sinai and found that the people had lapsed into
idolatry. The story of his blazing anger tells what a change had
come over the life of the people with the deliverance of "the

ten words," as Jews call them. No longer were the Israelites to put any images like the golden calf in place of the only, unseen God. He was a jealous God who wanted no human image in his place, nor the representation of sun or moon or beast of the earth or fish of the sea. Needless to say, graven images did not die out immediately in Israel. You find mention of them lingering on in the Books of Numbers (21:8f.), Judges (8:27), and 1 Kings (12:28ff.). Yet no representation of Israel's God, the LORD, has ever been found, nor of any wife or concubine or queen. He cannot be portrayed by any picture and has never had a partner.

The ten commandments are not a law code so much as a designation of the spirit underlying all the many laws that follow. They speak of the sanctity of God's being as shown forth by his name, of the sanctity of the seventh day devoted to worshipping him, of the sanctity of human life and marriage, property and good name. Israel's ethical requirements, unlike those of her neighbors, were rooted in God's will. He, the LORD, was holy. Fidelity to his commands was a simple matter of being like him. One came to resemble him by doing as he said.

An interesting thing took place as the Christian church gradually came to birth from the synagogue. The church showed very little interest in the ten commandments. To be sure, morality was important for the Christians of the early centuries. But they approached it by reading the biblical books in their entirety, not just concentrating on this list of ten "Thou shalts" and "Thou shalt nots." All through Lent in the third, fourth, and fifth centuries, the adults under instruction for baptism —catechumens, as they were called — were having their final preparation sessions. They had been living as

Christians in their conduct for two or three years. Now this was being solidified and summed up. The great stress was on the twofold law of love, so called: Jesus' command to love God with all one's heart and soul and strength and mind, and one's neighbor as oneself.

Just as Jesus, risen and dwelling in the church, came to be thought of as the new temple of God, so the two tablets of stone were thought to be summed up in the twofold command of Jesus. It was only Augustine in the early fifth century who brought the ten commandments into prominence in Christian instruction. He spoke of them as a ten-stringed lyre on which the Holy Spirit played, bringing the harmony of the divine order into our lives.

That is a beautiful way to look on the commandments. Their late use by the church is also important information for Christians who look on them as a new golden calf, an idol for adoration. There is a strange tendency to view them as the very heart of Christian behavior. But, of course, the Holy Spirit alone is that personal core. Without the Spirit, no conformity to God's will is possible. Apart from the Spirit at work within us, we do not expect to be able to keep these demands. Ethics or morality can become the great enemy — something outside ourselves that is too much for us — unless we come to have confidence in the Holy Spirit dwelling within who will make the whole venture possible. Jesus needs no one to give him testimony about human nature. He is well aware of what is in the human heart. Jesus has sent another Paraclete into our hearts to make conformity to his Father's will possible.

Lent is a time for personal reform. It is a season in which we hope to recapture the terms of our baptismal commitment.

Lent centers on God's folly and weakness in the stumbling block of the cross. Not our folly and our weakness which is the world's wisdom and strength. God's power and wisdom becomes our power and wisdom as we turn our backs on all the world holds dear.

We are not invited to be strong and wise in our personal lives only. It is a matter of reforming not only ourselves but the social institutions of which we are a part. We are called by the season of Lent to see what bad systems we are a willing part of, how our hearts are set on possessions even while we speak against the rich, how we resent the ills of society but in our heart of hearts contribute to them.

Repentance and reform is the message of Lent but not in individual hearts alone. It must take place throughout society, which is sick because it wants none of the power or wisdom of God. It does not want the cross but only its own weakness and folly.

March 25, 1973   Our Lady of Mercy Parish

THIRD SUNDAY OF LENT
Ex 3:1-8, 13-15; 1 Cor 10:1-6, 10-12; Lk 13:1-9/Year C

At our baptism, whenever it happened, we recited or our sponsors recited for us the Lord's prayer and the Apostles Creed. In the first prayer we were given God's proper name in our regard and we have been addressing him by it ever since. We called on God as "Father," even as Moses was given the name peculiar to God, YHWH, for which we substitute in speech "the LORD."

Jesus reports on two tragic occurrences well known to his hearers — the one an example of Pilate's cruelty as representative of the occupying power, the other a building accident in Jerusalem — and he calls for reform of life. Crudely put, Jesus' meaning is: "You are no better than the victims and perhaps a good deal worse, so shape up." Then Luke tempers this harsh judgment by juxtaposing a parable of mercy. The orchard keeper asks the owner to give the faltering fig tree a second chance. Jesus does not turn his story into an allegory so neither should we; I mean, by saying the owner is so-and-so, the farmer is so-and-so, and the fig tree is us. No, let us leave the tale as we find it — a powerful but generalized story of concern, clemency, and a fresh start.

It is the second selection from 1 Corinthians that probably brings home to us the lenten reality best of all. Read in isolation it can be thoroughly puzzling, but that is why homilies are suggested — to see what spiritual fruit we can derive from a sometimes puzzling "word of the Lord." The community in Corinth to which Paul had brought the gospel and where he had resided daily for eighteen months was in a state of spiritual anarchy. If the condition of the normal modern congregation is that it is largely dead but for a few active souls, the state of the Corinthian church was that it was jumping with life. Men and women were shouting in the assembly, the common weekly meal was chaotic — marked by drunkenness (11:21), and the sex lives of some were wildly out of line. All this in the name of religion. Nice religion, you might say. Any extra application blanks?

We are talking about a religious exaltation or enthusiasm going back to the Corinthians' pagan days which were not far behind them. "Enthusiasm," after all, means your favorite god in you and you in your god. You are taken over, possessed. You respond in excitement and frenzy. Perhaps you saw the Pope in Managua on Friday on television. He was trying to reduce the crowds to silence to invite them to a religious experience his style. They persisted in having a religious experience their style, shouting "La revoluci6n" and "Viva Jesús Cristo" with equal fervor. These were two expressions of the religious spirit on collision course. So, too, in Corinth. "I would remind you," St. Paul says, counting on their baptismal instruction still fresh in their memories, "about the journey of the Israelites across the Sinai." This must have been the backbone of their catechumenate on liberation from sin and slavery to freedom: passage through the sea with the pharaoh in hot pursuit, a pillar of cloud above them by day with the rock from which water was struck following them. That last is not in the Bible. It is legendary embroidering. "All for our instruction," says Paul. "All symbols of Christ." And the example given in Scripture, he says, was to teach this: that despite the favor of deliverance lavished on them some became idolators. They worshipped their wicked desires. In the name of religion they turned to lewdness, to such orgiastic play as the desert allowed. Their response was something like the original movie *M*A*S*H*, which was not at all like the relatively innocent TV serial. It was a black comedy about lust and ineffectual religion as two responses to the daily proximity to death in war.

To drive home his point St. Paul paints a graphic picture of debauchery by God's chosen ones during the exodus. His point is that there are none so strong they cannot fall. Religious advantages are no guarantee of fidelity. If you want to give in to your desires nothing can stop you.

Cut to 1983. Good family, Christian unbringing, a faithful spouse. Weakness, self-centeredness, passion — any one of them can bring the whole edifice crashing down. Any of us can make a tragic mockery of our baptism.

I do not for a moment suppose any of you is living a lurid life. Your temptations are different: sameness of schedule, pressure, the daily grind. But there is always alcohol only a liquor store away. There is beer or pot for young people or experimenting with sex if peer pressures prove stronger than a weak pattern of self-discipline in the home. There are all those release valves and others at hand — chiefly anger or sulking — to cope with what is too much for us. It may be a nagging parent for whom no measure of success in a child is good enough; a partner in marriage too committed to job or career to attend to spouse and family; a grouch, a wet blanket who makes all time spent outside the home more attractive than all time spent within it.

Paul was trying to wean his new converts from paganism away from a religious exaltation, a mad enthusiasm that was destroying them. If you know 1 Corinthians well you realize how much it is concerned with the boasting of "the strong" versus the spiritual timidity of "the weak." It was very much a class struggle, you deduce: the comfortable, the "haves," the spiritually sophisticated riding high over the "have nots." Being in a state of comfort is a good part of our problem, even as it was a good part of theirs. We do not have the troubles that come with living on Springfield or South Orange Avenue in Newark and we come to think we have earned the difference. Who do they think they are, wanting to live like us? We are the strong, they are the weak. We take things for granted. We looks for new experiences to add some spice to our lives. What is all the heavy drinking in the colleges about? Twelve thousand, next year thirteen thousand dollars a year at our academically best schools. And some young people in them blotto for two, three days out of seven. It happens at much cheaper rates of tuition, believe me. Lives without centers at twenty taking their cues from lives without centers at fifty.

I am probably talking into the wind. Maybe there is no parallel whatever between the Corinthian situation and ours, the spiritual and material "haves" and "have nots."

I know this much. There is a slump in every life when we forget the reasons for living which we have on file someplace. We need to recall whatever made us think carrying on was worthwhile. Lent is a time to remember, to ask ourselves, "If I had a chance to choose baptism on my own and live Christian, would I?"

To be a Christian in Jesus' sense is not to be religious. It is not to be moral. It is not to tend the garden of the soul, strive for perfection, look inward to check on spiritual progress. We are not that interesting, any of us. It is to live for God, which is to say to live the life of Jesus the man for others. For him life was service. He died because that is what it led to. He did not especially want to die. It was the logic of the situation. The church worldwide — any given congregation — is dead on the vine if it does only religious things, churchy things. It lives not to serve the church — itself — but the world.

Looking inward you can get into all sorts of bizarre behavior: like speaking in tongues, holding rallies in stadiums, banquets in hotels. It is all licking your own fur like a pussycat. We are the parish of X in the Diocese of Y and we did this, this, and that last year. And the poor, suffering human race came no closer to salvation.

God has so constructed the body as to give greater honor to the lowly members [Paul writes to Corinth], that there may be no dissension in the body, but that all the members may be concerned for one another. If one member suffers, all the other members suffer with it; if one member is honored, all the members share its joy.

We are coming on to mid-Lent. Try a family confab one day this week. With everybody there. Or three friends or neighbors if you do not live in a family. Ask what you have done to reach out to suffering members of the human race. How have you validated your baptism lately? It is an indelible character in the soul that says you care for the people only God worries about.

March 6, 1983   St. Joseph's Parish, Maplewood, NJ

FOURTH SUNDAY OF LENT
1 Sm 16:1, 6-7, 10-13; Eph 5:8-14; Jn 9:1-41/Year A

The word for baptism comes from a root that means "immerse" or "dip," even "dye" in the ancient world. Paul told the Galatians that baptism was a clothing in Christ (3:27) and the Romans that it was a burial with Christ after close association in his death (6:3-4). In the early Greek-speaking church, baptism came to be known as *phōtismōs*, an illumination or bath in light. John's gospel was a strong influence here — the word for light is *phōs* — as were other light-darkness passages in the correspondence of St. Paul. The phrase "sons of light" appears in John and in the *Manual of Discipline* from the Dead Sea community of separatist Jews. Today's gospel reading from John relates to the second selection from Ephesians more closely than to the first selection from 1 Samuel, which is unusual. But in Advent and Lent all three readings are tailored to one theme whereas on ordinary Sundays selections one and three form the poles of an axis while the second reading goes its own way.

The main concern of this Sunday for many centuries has been the impending baptism of adults into the congregation on the Great Night of Easter. The choice of David, the unprepossessing shepherd boy, by Israel's God is a parable of the mystery of our election. Why, of the billions on the earth, have we been chosen? Our personal merits are all against it, just as in the world's eyes the raw lad David was no match for the regal Saul. Ephesians names the conditions of the new life of the baptized throughout Chapter 5, from which we read. It culminates in what may well be a snatch from an early baptismal hymn: "Awake, O sleeper, arise from the dead and Christ will give you life" (Eph 5:14). We the baptized hope that we are awake and alive in the light that is Christ. We have no need to put a cover of darkness over our shameful deeds.

An obscure seventeenth-century poet named John Denham wrote these lines in a poem called *Progress of Learning*:

I can no more believe old Homer blind,
Than those who say the sun hath never shined;
The age wherein he lived was dark, but he
Could not want sight who taught the world to see.

Those lines say something very important about the ancient, sightless bard. The gospels used the imagery of blindness and vision to signify spiritual resistance and openness to truth long

before the English poet thought to do so. Every cure of
blindness by Jesus reported in the gospels is used as a parable
of opening the eyes of the mind in faith. To be united with
Christ in baptism is to see the world as it is, not to impose a
false character on it stemming from our talent for self-
deception. To live as a Christian, in a word, is to see.

Easter is three weeks away. It will celebrate the baptism of
some absolutely new Christians in our midst and the reception of others into our ancient Catholic communion. We who
are Catholics must be sighted people to receive them. Otherwise it will be the blind leading the blind and their last state
will be worse than the first. We remember the scorn Jesus
poured on those who traveled over sea and land to make a
single proselyte and we ask, "Is it we, Lord?"

Why do people speak today of the wisespread loss of hope
in these United States, of our purposelessness as a people, our
lack of direction? Our country is so good to some, so cruel to
others. Yet it is by no means the case that the favored see
meaning in their lives while the disfavored do not. Often it is
just the opposite. There is no correlation whatever between
possessions or good fortune and a sense of purpose.

Getting very specific, do we who claim the Christian name
in a community of believers, a church, know where we are
going? That is the question for Lent — in a sense, the only
question for Lent.

Jesus quizzed the man who was blind from birth: "Do you
believe in the son of man?" (Jn 9:35). One wonders if this was
a direct question put to the candidates in the rite of baptism in
the Johannine community, perhaps the only question. Jesus
asks another question in Matthew: "What do you want me to
do for you?" and the two who are blind answer: "Lord, open
our eyes" (Mt 20:32f.).

The invitation to life in the church in a particular congregation is a call to a lifetime of clear sight regarding the son of man. Christian life is more. It is the life of vision regarding all humanity or it is nothing.

In our day people, even Christian people, are terribly wary of one another. There is a profound lack of trust. The fear is not so much that deeds of darkness will be uncovered but that the deep inadequacy in each of us will come to light. "Dare I level with him?" "Why should I tell her the whole truth?" "I doubt they will be honest with me."

The fourth gospel's "son of man" in whom the evangelist required belief was that unspeakable paradox, a weak human being in whom the *full* glory of God shone forth. The venture of faith has not changed since then. God is not in others exactly as God is in Jesus; nonetheless, God is very much in others. Do we dare to look at them? Have we the courage to show forth the divine glory that is in us or will we, clutching our human weakness, keep it from others' gaze until we die?

Catholics and many other Christians zealously guard the custom of christening in infancy. Those committed to a "believer's baptism" wait until adolescence, until adulthood. In a sense, by its practice neither tradition asks the deepest question.

The question is: Are Christians such a community of trust that one would wish passionately to be of their number? Is joining them a new life or is it just a bit of ritual behavior, an accident of birth, in some circles a Bible-spouting *about* a new life? These are lenten questions.

"Great God! I'd rather be/ A Pagan suckled in a creed outworn," said the Christian Wordsworth. Than what? Than getting and spending. Than living comfortably with "the world." Than not *seeing* what is there to be seen.

Do we really want anyone to join us in our faith community three weeks from now? Does it mean that much to us? Will is ever? These are lenten questions. We have three weeks to answer.

March 29, 1981   St. James Church

FOURTH SUNDAY OF LENT
2 Chr 36:14-17, 19-23; Eph 2:4-10; Jn 3:14-21/Year B

Genuine celebrations — whether they be liturgies or family meals or parties — must grow out of life. They must help people return to life with deeper understanding, renewed strength, and invigorated hope.

For you who come regularly to an early Sunday Mass the word "celebration" may not seem an apt one — even though you are familiar with the phrase "celebrate Mass." Some congregations and presiding priests "celebrate" the Eucharist while others simply participate in the ancient rite. Celebration to be celebration need not be raucous or noisy; it need not even have song (although nothing is quite so helpful in celebrating as song). But celebration must have some element of joy, however somber the occasion — the death of Jesus for our sins, the funeral Mass of a beloved friend, even the need to fulfill a weekly duty of prayer on a bleak morning. You cannot celebrate without some joy.

Ours is a quiet joy at this early hour: that God has made us in the divine image and made us good; that God has given to the world the only Son Jesus Christ, perfect image of the love

God bears us; that the gifts of life and hope are ours so long as there is a breath left in us — a world to redeem and a personal task to perform in that massive undertaking. It is twenty past seven on the first day of spring. It is three weeks short of the Easter feast that is our salvation. It is the lenten Sunday that used to be called *"Laetare"* from its entrance hymn from Isaiah 66 (10):

> Rejoice with Jerusalem and be glad because of her,
>   all you who love her;
> Exult, exult with her,
>   all you who were mourning over her....
> For...I will spread prosperity over her like a river,
>   and the wealth of nations like a torrent....
> As a mother comforts her child so shall I comfort you;
>   in Jerusalem you shall find your comfort.

To be Christian is to find our comfort in Jerusalem. What does that mean?

The Chronicler, as we call the author of the first reading, is a severe moralist. He re-tells the story from 2 Kings of Jerusalem's fall to the Babylonians under Nebuchadnezzar in 587; he does so by explaining Israel's defeat theologically. The city has been besieged and put to the torch, he says, because King Zedekiah resisted the advice of Jeremiah and all God's messengers and prophets during his eleven-year reign. The captivity will end in seventy years, the Chronicler has Jeremiah say, when the land "retrieves its lost sabbaths," that is, when it keeps them faithfully. It is a little bit like my telling you that we can stave off nuclear war by keeping Sunday piously, otherwise God's wrath will descend upon us through a bomb attack that will destroy us.

I do not have a theology of cause and effect like that. I hope you do not either. A just nation, a peace-loving nation may expect that no tragedies will overtake it in punishment for its sins — sins of greed, of munitions sales, of oppression of the helpless. But there is no Christian theology which teaches that social and personal morality can keep a people from all harm. There is too much evidence that the innocent suffer, that bystanders — whether persons or nations — can be snuffed out when they are guilty of no social evil whatever.

What we do have in our Christian faith, because it is biblical faith, is the conviction of a relation between the death of the Lamb and a world's sin. From Adam's day there has been rebellion, from Cain's day murder, from Lamech's day senseless revenge. The sum of human guilt is staggering. At times it can be established who did what to whom: the genocide of the Indians by Europeans in both Americas which still goes on; the death of innocents of all ages by drunken drivers, young and old; the holocaust of Jews, Slavs, and Gypsies by the Nazis because of perverted theories of racial purity.

At other times, though, the tangle of human sin is such that no guilt for tragedies can be directly established. This complexity of motives and non-motives and chance has led us Christians to avoid trying to play God and frame a simple formula. We turn instead to a revealed insight that comes to us from the apostolic age and is found in the New Testament. The weight of human guilt, which is the fruit of disobedience, can only be removed by the obedience of one human creature, the perfectly obedient Jesus.

In today's gospel we are told that the whole world is healed in Jerusalem, the city of peace. For the Israelites there had been death in the desert through snakes, those cleverest of beasts. There is life for all humanity outside the city walls of Jerusalem through Jesus who said we must be as clever as serpents. The son of man must be lifted up from earth — in crucifixion, in resurrection, for John it is the same deed of glory — that all who believe may have eternal life in him. Sin's power over us is literally too much for us. There is a terrible price to pay for it, we know, and it has already been paid. The price is perfect conformity to God's will.

And so I tell you to rejoice with Jerusalem this early lenten morning. It is "the city of the great King," as Jesus said. It is the place of our salvation. For, although Jesus died there, it is a city of life. There is no condemnation for us if we believe what God accomplished for us in him.

God chose us there to be blameless, to be full of love. "It is in Christ and through his blood that we have been redeemed and our sins forgiven" (Eph 1:7). "God . . . brought us to life in Christ when we were dead in sin. By this grace you were saved" (2:5). Indeed we do have something to celebrate, despite the early hour and the numbness of our recent rising from sleep. "We are truly [God's] handiwork created in Christ Jesus to live a life of good deeds. . . ." (v. 10).

Sin is powerful, it is true, destroying nations, leveling cities, corrupting lives. But grace and faith in the resurrection are more powerful still. So in your quiet way at this memorial meal, celebrate! Rejoice with Jerusalem and be glad because of her.

March 21, 1982   St. Paul's Parish, 7:00 AM

FOURTH SUNDAY OF LENT
Josh 5:9a, 10-12; 2 Cor 5:17-21; Lk 15:1-3, 11-32 /Year C

On March 12 in the year 295 a young man named Maximilian refused induction into the army at Theveste in the North African province of Numidia in modern Algeria. The Roman proconsul of Africa reminded him that other Christians were soldiers but he would not give in and so was executed.

On July 21, 298, a centurion named Marcellus publicly renounced his military oath. Three months later he was put to death by the vicar of the provinces of Spain.

Why did these men act as they did? We do not know. There were two emperors at the time, Diocletian and Maximian, one Eastern-based in Sirmium now in Hungary, the other Western in the German town of Trier. Diocletian had erected a colossal statue of the sun god at Sirmium and put himself under the protection of Jupiter. Maximian did the same with Hercules. Was that the reason we had these early martyrs — refusal of the military oath to emperors who identified themselves with gods? Or was the reason killing in war? The acts of their martyrdoms do not say.

This much we know. The government expenditures of the time, both military and civil, were immense. They led to increased taxation and inflated currency. Diocletian we are told "would never permit the treasury to be diminished" and "his various evildoings produced enormously high prices." Grain became scarce, black market speculators flourished. In 301 he tried to stop the runaway price spiral by fixing both wages and prices. He spoke of the past favor shown to Rome by the immortal gods and insisted that people practice the state religion so that prosperity might return. But because of people's fears no goods appeared on the market and prices soared. In 302 Diocletian's number two man, Galerius, supported by several military advisers, argued that Christianity had to be suppressed. Why did the emperor forbid it among court officials and the army? Because Christians would not venerate the emperors as gods? Probably not. Probably because the war was going badly, because taxpayers were groaning under enormous assessments, because a scapegoat was needed on whom to fix the blame. What if Maximilian and Marcellus *were* men of excellent character? They were against the government. That was reason enough to still their voices.

Last week in Baltimore the 209 delegates of the National Federation of Priests' Councils, representing sixty percent of the country's dioceses, did "hereby unhesitatingly condemn the continuation of the United States' involvement in the war in Southeast Asia." They called the war "the most serious moral issue of the time." They opposed extension of the present draft system when the Selective Service Act expires June 30, contending that it has given the president the power to induct an unlimited number of men "without the salutary effect of an annual review in Congress." The federation opposed the creation of a compulsory national service core as an alternative to the draft. They accused J. Edgar Hoover of "premature and unfortunate allegations" in the Berrigan case, inappropriate because they presume guilt rather than innocence before trial which is contrary to the American system of justice.

A month ago a committee of the Federation on Human Resources and Development had declared the [Berrigan] Harrisburg charges "not nearly as alarming as the fact that the

United States today commits half of its resources to militarism and tolerates poverty as a way of life for millions of its citizens."

When we read about the persecutions of Decius and Diocletian we tend to think that they were chiefly about incense offered to idols and the military oath to the emperor as a god. But of course they were not. They were about big government, big spending, big bloodletting and big taxation to achieve glory for the few. They were about a tiny handful of religious believers who thought that things had gone far enough. The parallels between the years 300 and 1971 are very close indeed.

One of the co-conspirators named in the Harrisburg case is like Henry Kissinger a German-born Jew who came here in the thirties to escape Hitler. Kissinger became a Harvard professor, Paul Meyer a Benedictine monk of Newton Abbey in New Jersey. He is no longer a monk but a Catholic layman. Three weeks ago he said publicly: "We both came to this country to escape the kind of thing that Mr. Kissinger is helping to perpetrate, namely, a huge, impersonal system which sets aside the rights of a whole people."

Needless to say no government can endure the kind of criticism this one is receiving before it reacts angrily to retaliate. In the Roman Empire one technique used was the setting of fires of mysterious origin, with dark hints that the Christians were behind them. Another was insistence on induction into the army; for refusal, death.

On Friday the House Armed Services Committee voted to eliminate draft deferments for divinity students and to extend the required civilian service for conscientious objectors to three years from two. The elimination of deferments would not apply to men who now hold them but none would be granted in the future. The administration has wanted this change and Committee Chairman F. Edward Hébert of Louisiana sponsored it only too willingly. Earlier last week the Committee voted to abolish future deferments for all college undergraduates except ROTC members. Two weeks ago the Supreme Court decided that the only conscientious objectors who should be heard were those who oppose all wars and not just a single conflict.

A number of legislators have favored the end of deferments for college students lest the poor and the unschooled be the ones to die in all wars. The clergy are another matter. In World Wars I and II religion was thought to be good for the country. The clergy at home supported our wars; in the field they helped the troops to die. Now the clergy are taking the commandment "Thou shalt not kill" more seriously. They are not the whole peace movement by any means but they are a particularly vocal part of it. They begin — very slowly, very tentatively — to be an anti-government force as Christians were in Diocletian's day. But that is not chiefly what they are about. They begin to heed St. Paul when he writes, "God has reconciled us to himself through Christ and has given us the ministry of reconciliation . . . he has entrusted the message of reconciliation to us."

March 21, 1971   Our Lady of Mercy Parish

FIFTH SUNDAY OF LENT
Ez 37:12-14; Rom 8:8-11; Jn 11:1-45/Year A

"I have promised it and I will do it, says the LORD" (Ez
37:14). What has he promised and what has he by now done?
A restoration of the people Israel under the figure of the
resurrection of the dead; that is what he has accomplished. But
the vision of the dry bones is not really about the dead coming
back to life — sinews put back, flesh restored, bones coming
together, bone joining bone. The vision of Ezekiel is about the
Jews back in their homeland starting fresh. "See, I will bring
spirit into you, that you may come to life . . . and know that I
am the LORD" (5-6).

The story of Lazarus in John's gospel is a story about the
resuscitation of a dead man. But is it? "Lazarus, come out."
Come out of what? The stench of the sepulcher, the progress
toward dust already begun? Not really, although there is no
reason to deny that wonder in Jesus' career. St. John is
interested in a wonder greater still. "Whoever believes in me
will never die" (11:26); so, "Untie him and let him go free," is
a word of freedom from many things besides the grave-cloths
of burial custom. It too is a release from human bondage, like
that of Ezekiel's many bones strewn on the surface of the
plain. John never means as little as he says, even when the
"little" is a marvel in a world where death and the grave take a
universal toll.

"Those who are in the flesh cannot please God," we hear
from Paul (Rom 8:8). "But you are not in the flesh; you are in
the spirit, since the spirit of God dwells in you" (v. 9). Now
we are getting down to cases. All three readings from the Bible
mean one thing, that the LORD is not a God of dead souls, a

people in bondage, but of a living, active humanity that lives for him. They are lenten readings, of course; hence the immediate reference is baptismal. The Holy Spirit that energizes the baptismal bath is the sign of power of the new eon. The old age — "flesh" Paul calls it, meaning human resistance to God's call — is over. The bones on the plain, the dead Lazarus wept and mourned for, are the perfect signs of an eon past. But that time is over or can be in a community of believers. Its successor is an age of spirit — mortal bodies brought to life through "God's spirit dwelling in you." That indeed bespeaks the hope of future resurrection, but its primary referent is other. As in the days of the sixth century prophet, St. Paul cares chiefly about a people now alive. The church is not a community forever exploring the biblical past. It is not fixed on thoughts of the future, important though they are. Its great concern is spirit now, life now. It is committed to the superiority of a life lived for God over living death.

Yesterday I spent some time with a friend I meet only infrequently. He is a layman who has spent much of his life as an editor but is now teaching English in a Catholic college in Suburban Sprawl, NY — 10,000 students in a dozen locations in a single county. He says that these students, for the most part, cannot conceive religion as anything but the Catholic religion, a religion they profess but do not practice. Sunday Mass attendance is very low, the Jews of New Testament times were in a state of bad faith for not accepting Jesus, and Catholic faith consists in "being good." I put that phrase in quotation marks because it means avoiding the major vices and the list is somewhat selective. Now, you will not hear ethical uprightness scorned from this lectern but I hope I know enough — like my professor friend — to distinguish between it and discipleship of Jesus.

To follow Jesus is to live for God, to seek God's will and do it. Being Christian is a profoundly religious act. Moral behavior is the fruit of it but the main thing is admitting the Spirit, the totality of godhead, into one's being. It is living as if God were the greatest reality in life, for this alone can assure our taking the world, our humanity, the fact of *now*, seriously.

We delight in speaking of the life of the baptized as a new life and so it is. But we need to be clear what we mean when we say that. The same is true of a phrase that rolls from the Catholic tongue, "supernatural life." In common parlance supernatural means "spooky," "eerie." Not to us. It is another word for life in the Spirit, God's spirit dwelling in you. Still, there are hazards. Of these the chief is the possibility that we become convinced that there is ordinary life, real life and then some kind of religious addition from another sphere, perhaps basically after death or in the future. The last stop on the line is a depreciation of this life in favor of that, the code words being "supernatural: good," "natural: bad."

Jesus knew nothing of a life that was bad, only the distinct possibility of misspending life. Paul's "flesh" was not ordinary, everyday life; it was a life of disobedience, a life lived in revolt. For us who bear the name Christian, the life of faith is ordinary life headed in the direction God intends. It is the whole creation redeemed, that is, oriented in a Godward direction. Grace is letting God accomplish all he means to be and do in us. The life of Christian belief is life at its most reasonable, not unreasonable or non-reasonable.

So think and pray hard these next two weeks about what it means to be called to such a life. Do you want it, really want it, or is being Catholic merely a matter of old habit? Would you be *redeemed*, reborn in water and Holy Spirit? Then prepare for the Easter season rejoicing, not lugubrious at the death of Jesus, not straining to recapture childhood practices about Passiontide, but repentant in joy and confident in the merciful justice of God.

April 5, 1981   St. David the King Church

FIFTH SUNDAY OF LENT
Jer 31:31-34; Heb 5:7-9; Jn 12:20-33/Year B

There is an American black poet named Gwendolyn Brooks who has written a short poem called "The Pool Players. Seven at the Golden Shovel." It goes like this:

We real cool. We
Left school. We

Lurk late. We
Strike straight. We

Sing sin. We
Thin gin. We

Jazz June. We
Die soon.

It is hard for us to keep in mind that Jesus of Nazareth was a young man who died soon. Martin Luther King, Jr., whose anniversary of death was on Monday, lived to be thirty-nine.

Jesus probably didn't last that long. We forget that his widowed mother buried this victim of Roman violence and was left with her memories of how good a boy he had been, like many another since her time. He was a preacher of peace but the authorities of the Empire took him for one more Jewish nationalist, one more freedom fighter, and that was the end of him. "Judicial murder," we call it nowadays — falling afoul of the government in power with your convictions about the abuse of power in full view.

The second and third readings today, as we come on toward Easter, are about Jesus troubled at the prospect of suffering, Jesus facing the reality of death and not finding it inviting. The second reading from the letter to the Hebrews provides the New Testament's clearest picture of Jesus suffering as one of us, "in the days of his flesh" (v. 7). They contain this explanation of the way our salvation was accomplished: once perfected by the obedience he had learned from what he suffered, Christ became the cause of eternal salvation for those obedient to him. The obedience we are called to is in the same order as his. He saves us by his example but in a more direct way still. His obedience to God makes it possible for us to be obedient. Jesus' "loud cries and tears" were the sign that he faced the implications of accepting God's will perfectly.

In what sense was God able to save him from death when in fact God did not? And how was he heard because of his reverence? The author of Hebrews cannot have the passion in mind. He must be thinking of the reverent stance of Jesus throughout his life that saved him in every instance but the last. "Son though he was, he learned obedience from what he suffered. . . ." This sonship of God provided him with no immunity from suffering but equipped him in a special way

for the high priestly office to which he was called. This is a
theology of being tried and passing the test. It locates Christ's
power to save us, not in his divine status, but in his perseverance through pain as an obedient man.

The gospel spells out the same theme though much more
calmly — quite unlike the reference to the passion in
Hebrews with its "prayers and supplications, loud cries and
tears." It reports Jesus' temptation to pray for deliverance
—"Father, save me from this hour" — but also his rejection
of that temptation. When he speaks to the Greeks who
approach him at the feast, probably proselyte Jews from
paganism, he does so in terms of the coming hour of his
glorification, of life through death, of "loving" one's life and
losing it versus "hating" it and keeping it. The evangelist John
cannot remain for long within the earthly life of Jesus; he has
to get into the lives of believers. "If anyone serves me/ him the
Father will honor," he has Jesus say. In other words, the
glorification of the individual will be God's response to human
faithfulness, just as in the passion, "The hour has come/ for
the Son of Man to be glorified."

These two readings are indicative of the two main ways of
looking at Jesus' death on the cross for our redemption. One
stresses the hardship of his being obedient to the point of
death, the other emphasizes the glory of the outcome. That, in
turn, underlies the difficulty we have in taking the mystery of
the cross seriously. It happened a long time ago to someone
else. Besides he got out of it like Houdini, whom they couldn't
keep in any padlock or strait-jacket. But the reality of death as
we know it is something different. It is a thief, robbing us of all
those we love best. It is often cruel to the one who dies. And it
is final.

Edna St. Vincent Millay wrote a poem called "The Conscientious Objector" in defiance of death:

> I will not tell him the
> whereabouts of my friends nor
> of my enemies either.
> Though he promise me much, I will
> not map him the route to any
> man's door.
> Am I a spy in the land of the living,
> that I should deliver men to death?

She has another poem, speaking the thoughts of a wife and mother whose husband has left her and the children:

> Listen, children:
> Your father is dead.
> From his old coats
> I'll make you little jackets.
> I'll make you little trousers
> From his old pants....
>
> Life must go on,
> And the dead be forgotten;
> Life must go on,
> Though good men die;
> Anne, eat your breakfast;
> Dan, take your medicine;
> Life must go on;
> I forget just why.

We have let the mystery of the resurrection do a strange thing to us in our preaching in the church. We have let it block out the harshness of death. But such was never Jesus' intent.

He was tempted to ask to be saved from this hour. He faced it, not without a loud outcry and tears. When it came judgment came on this world. Jesus was no spy in the land of the living that he should deliver himself to death.

No, he died that life would come of it. He died to give his sisters and brothers a new heart and a new spirit; he died to place God's law within them and write it on their hearts.

I heard a splendid, brief tribute to Dr. King one night last week on the radio. It was by a newsman named Herbert Caplow, who spoke as if he had been in his company often and knew him well. He said that Dr. King never went the way of flamboyance, never capitalized on his popularity or acted the demagogue. King knew the power of his oratory; he was never in doubt about that. But he didn't use it as a tool for self-advancement, let alone for racism or hatred. He was a great leader, said the commentator, not only of black people but of white people as well — a towering human resource during a time of great national crisis.

Do we glorify the assassination of that great figure? Surely we do not, any more than we take delight in the death of Jesus. To do so would be scarcely human but, rather, perverse. No, we look on death as the enemy — the more so when hatred or a twisted mentality has brought it on. The only thing that must die is pretense, pose, phoniness. The unreal self must die. The real self must live. All the energy that has been devoted to keeping up a front, to hatred among brothers can now be given to life, to reality.

"Father, do not let the prince of this world prevail but glorify your name!"

April 8, 1973   Our Lady of Mercy Parish

FIFTH SUNDAY OF LENT
Is 43:16-21; Phil 3:8-14; Jn 8:1-11/Year C

Lent is a time for renewal. That means that we ought to face certain questions during its course as we come on to Easter's climax. We hope to celebrate the new person and renewed commitment to what it means to be baptized. We can only do that in good conscience, though, if we learn how to handle our past. We have to discover how to carry it, bear it, for the past is a burden we cannot lay down. Our past is part of us whether we like it or not. It is part of our lives and inescapable.

The strange thing is that when you read the Bible on the subject of conversion or change of heart you are invited not only to move ahead but actively and consciously to repudiate the past: "Wipe it out, forget it." That is what the Scripture says. Not just the bad and regrettable things but the good things as well; the good things especially. They provide the heaviest weight of all so over the side they have to go.

Take today's readings, for example:

Remember not the events of the past,
    the things of long ago consider not;
See, I am doing something new!
    Now it springs forth, do you not perceive it?
In the desert I make a way,
    in the wasteland, rivers.

That passage was meant to have a forceful impact on the Jewish community of the time after the exile. What it said was: "The deliverance from Egypt, the whole Sinai business? Forget it! This is a fresh start." The past can be a terrible burden, especially when it was a successful past. So the biblical author does a bold thing by quoting God against himself. The One who snuffed out chariots and horsemen like a wick, laying them prostrate in the Red Sea never to rise, now tells his people to remember none of this. He wants them to look ahead to the new situation, the return from Babylon. The talk about water in the desert and rivers in the wasteland is about a journey westward to Jerusalem, not eastward from Egypt. The reason God is made to speak this way is clear. Whenever Israel begins to reminisce about her greatness there is more worth forgetting than remembering.

Would you have me remember, have us come to trial? (v. 26)

A bad bargain, says the LORD. You remember a way through the Red Sea but I remember sins and crimes.

It is I, I, who wipe out . . . your offenses;
your sins I remember no more. (v. 25)

In order to be new men and women, therefore, we have to repudiate our past and especially our past glories. The church is a pilgrim church, not a settler. Its own past can be an awful, crushing burden. The liberation Jesus provides involves repudiation of our "religious" past as well as of our "secular" past.

My car battery went dead one Sunday morning two months ago, a discovery I made at half past eleven. So I raced to the Thirtieth Street Station and caught a cab. The driver knew north Philadelphia well. When he saw that "Broad and Susquehanna" meant that I was coming to Our Lady of Mercy he began to confide in me — two white fellow-conspirators who had a secret: "I used to live here when I was a boy," he said, naming the corner. "They call it a ghetto. Believe me it was no ghetto then. Why this used to be the richest parish in Philadelphia." I said, "We've improved things a lot since then. It's no good when the churches are rich, is it?" Absolute silence until we arrived at this corner. I'd stolen a line right out of the Bible and invited him to forget the successes of his religious past. He didn't like the notion any better than I would if he had asked me to give up something equally dear to me.

St. Paul says he has come to consider his whole religious past rubbish so that Christ can be his wealth: circumcision, observance of the law, membership in the tribe of Benjamin — he wants to forget it. Consider what that means. That would be as if you and I were to say, not, "All the Catholic schools, all the religious orders, all the people at the consecration of a bishop," but rather, "My baptism, all the times I went to communion, the Fridays I didn't eat meat, the birth control I never practiced — all rubbish 'in the light of the surpassing knowledge of my Lord Jesus Christ.' " It is not our sinful past that is our great enemy but out religious past which has become an unconscious boast.

Oscar Wilde says somewhere, "He was a good man in the worst sense of that word." That's you and me in need of Easter renewal. We come to suppose that there is nothing in the biblical message that could offend a person of good faith, a sincere person, someone like us.

That is not the case. The gospel is offensive. It cuts across the grain, not with it. It asks us to be new.

A couple of weeks ago some legislation was promulgated in our church which said that priests who had left priestly service, whether by way of dispensation from their obligation or not, were under no condition to be allowed to preach or teach theology in seminaries or celebrate the sacraments. The directive sounded so unlike the Jesus of this morning's gospel it was frightening. It was the very thing we have been speaking about — clinging to our religious past as if it were life's supreme good. The argument in the case of the priests runs: "The people would be scandalized." Scandalized to hear again the voice in the box of the kindest confessor they ever had, to see at the altar the man who most embodied Christ to them in a long life of searching for him. People don't take scandal at things like that but at the heartless pride of men who say: "We represent virtue. We're still on the job reeking of fidelity."

The scribes and the Pharisees are the problem in this morning's gospel, not the woman. Remember who the scribes and Pharisees were. They were ordinary good men, religious men, the faithful ones. They were in love with all the good things in Israel's history, especially with the Law. They were in love with all that was good in the past.

They were not being asked by Jesus to approve of adultery but only to live in the present, to be *with* the woman now. "Then the audience drifted away one by one, beginning with the elders."

Who can take it? Who can stand it — this challenge to be new? It really is not a matter of "changes in the church" at all. That has nothing to do with it. It is the challenge of Jesus not to idolize our own past, to change constantly, and the church learning again for the thousandth thousandth time what Jesus is up to.

"I give no thought to what lies behind but push on to what is ahead," says Paul. "My entire attention is on the finish line."

We cannot put our past behind us like a snake shedding its skin or a bird its feathers. That is impossible. But for our children's sake we can and must cease clinging to a dead past, a past of religious achievement. Christ was above all else an apostle not of tradition but of change. The first change takes place in ourselves. When we are changing we do not resent and resist change in institutions, in ways of doing things. We rather expect it to happen. As disciples of Jesus we have no other choice.

March 28, 1971 Our Lady of Mercy Parish

PASSION SUNDAY
Is 50:4-7; Phil 2:6-11; Mt 27:11-54/Year A

It is helpful at certain seasons of the year to recall what we are about when we gather for our weekly celebration. Today, Passion Sunday, is such a day.

We come here to pray. We do not come to prove anything in particular to God or ourselves nor to establish our virtue but to appear before him who gives us life, to thank him for the gift of salvation. We do it today with palm branches as the special sign, though bread and wine are the ordinary symbols every Sunday.

Salvation means "saving" and the saving it means is total. It is not only being saved from the consequences of our sins, although that is part of it. It is being saved from death and disease and accident, saved from a life worse than the one we live, saved from a drowning at high tide once a day. The important thing about our being saved or spared is that it happens because someone was *not* spared. "Death is at work in us but life in you," Paul wrote long ago (2 Cor 4:12). He meant that the apostles died daily so as to transmit the gift of life. It was possible to do so because Christ had died before them for the same purpose. His death is our life.

What does this mean, his death is our life? Is it true in the politician's sense, who says in defense of his own willfulness and stupidity that the sons of the people shall not have died in vain? Is it true in the patriot's sense, who says that a thousand thousand deaths are worth it to make us a nation once again? Is it true in the hero's sense, who gives his life that his people may know peace and freedom? No, Jesus' death is neither a bargain with heaven nor a gamble nor a calculated risk. Above all, it is not the slaughter of a brave young man engineered by God to excite our pity.

It is God's gift to us of a perfectly obedient life — God's putting at our disposal the consequences of a life lived so well that all the mean-spiritedness of all the ages, the human disobedience of the centuries, *had* to snuff it out. Sin had no choice but to destroy it. Yet so powerful was this human life that the sum total of human sinfulness could only be conquered by it, not conquer it. The full tale of hatred from Cain until now is as nothing compared to the love of this life that ended in death.

Isaiah wrote centuries ago about a sufferer who would speak a word to the weary that would rouse them, a man who would give his body up to be beaten, having set his face like flint. This mysterious servant knew nothing of shame or disgrace. He had put his trust in God his help. The well-trained tongue with which he spoke was given him by God.

Many years later, those who believed that Jesus fulfilled the image of this ancient sufferer wrote a hymn in praise of him as the heavenly Adam who waived his rights. They doubtless sang it at their weekly gatherings like ours, even as they ate the meal in which they remembered him:

> He emptied himself
>> and took the form of a slave . . .
> known to be of human estate . . .
>> [though he was in the form of God]
>> he humbled himself,
> obediently accepting even death, death on a cross!
> Because of this, God exalted him on high
>> and bestowed on him the name
>> above every other name. . . .

The deepest meaning of our weekly assembly is that it unfolds the meaning of our lives to us in terms of the life of another. We see slaughter in our neighborhoods, the eighth-grade boys of a few years ago strung out on drugs; real estate men, landlords and food market owners growing rich at the expense of the poor. The spectacle of 30,000 children marching in the nation's capital yesterday was called "degrading," when one might have thought that the need of their parents to live on welfare was what was degrading. Our whole existence is a spectacle of death in the midst of life. The story of Jesus' passion is a spectacle of life in the midst of death.

That is why we do not have time to waste on Sunday on things like modesty in dress or distractions in prayer or the commandments of the church. "Someone's dyin', Lord, cumbaya." That someone is everyone, and only the death of Christ on the cross has anything to say to it.

Yesterday a group of thirty-three Catholic theologians, beginning with a group of five in Germany, published a statement "Against Discouragement in the Church." A Canadian friend invited me so I am one of them. A Swiss priest wrote it. It says that "the present crisis in the Church can be overcome only if the total Christian community, pope, bishops, pastors, theologians, and laity, lay hold anew of the Church's own center and foundation: the gospel of Jesus Christ. . . . It is not programs that are needed today but their living out." The statement says that on many issues the Church does not,

— in the judgment of friends and adversaries alike — follow the footsteps of Him to whom she constantly appeals. For this reason a curious contrast can be noticed today between great interest in Jesus and an utter lack of interest in the Church . . . . Freedom is demanded for the Church outside, but it is not granted inside. Justice and peace are preached, so long as the Church and its leaders do not have to pay the cost. Secondary issues are fought for while the total, future-oriented vision and clear priorities are neglected.

It is not worth our while to gather on a Sunday and eat the body of the Lord if, while doing so, we deplore the sins of others. They are not here to be preached to. They may, in fact, repent and change their ways but it will not be because of anything they heard in Our Lady of Mercy Church. It is we ourselves whom we must confront with the meaning of the gospel, not distant leaders in Washington, Saigon and Hanoi, or Rome. Tomorrow morning at work or school you and I will resume our customary roles as members of a church that fights for secondary issues — I make an exception of abortion, which is not a secondary issue — that wants freedom for everyone but its own laity and clergy. The statement I quoted from says on this point, referring to the responsibilities of the writers:

> The demands of the gospel along with the needs and hopes of our time are in many important questions so unambiguous, so clear, that silence out of opportunism, lack of courage, or superficiality makes one just as guilty as those responsible persons who were silent during the time of the Reformation.

We may not be silent over the many clear issues that confront us. If we are silent, we have lost the right to celebrate the passion of Christ, the innocent sufferer. The name of that technique is selective justice. We Christians have been adept at it for too long a time.

A week ago yesterday, the Reverend Jesse Jackson of Chicago made this appeal. (Incidentally, his ungrammatical speech is a means to identify with his hearers. A colleague at Temple who taught him at the Chicago Theological Seminary says he was one of the best students ever enrolled there.)

> When I look around and see the 50 million hungry — 34 million of them white — they ain't got nobody feeding them a meal, just feeding them Jim Crow . . . whether it is Hanrahan, Wallace, or Nixon, they're just feeding them Jim Crow. . . .

This country today needs jobs and income . . . . It needs health care. It needs medicine. It needs peace and nonracism. Jim Crow is not a substitute . . . .The issue in 1972 is not to save your party, not even your pride, but to save the union.

Is it important to us to celebrate the institution of the Holy Eucharist this Thursday? I am sure it is. Our Lord's death this Friday, burial on Saturday, resurrection on Sunday? I am equally sure. We may not *not* observe them. But there is a condition. We are not allowed the luxury of crocodile tears: lamenting a death that is far from us while conspiring in other deaths that are near. We may not say, "Let's keep religion and politics separate," when they were so intertwined in the passion and death of Christ. He did not hang on a cross simply because of some theological abstraction known as sin. He hung there because the fruit of sin took the form of power people fearing the peace movement he represented, because they did not want to lose income or power, because keeping the Jews in subjection meant prosperity to the rich Roman colonials. You can see it, can you not? The voice of the poor *had* to be silenced.

I guess I am saying that you and I have to earn the right to celebrate Holy Week.

March 26, 1972　　　　　　　　Our Lady of Mercy Parish

PASSION SUNDAY
Is 50:4-7; Phil 2:6-11; Mk 14:1—15:47/Year B

Spoken before the gospel

The question raised by today's Scripture readings is fairly simple: Why must the innocent suffer? What sense do death and bloodshed make?

The reading from Isaiah poses the problem, Philippians provides a solution in the reaches of eternity, and the passion of Christ according to Mark lies somewhere in between. The prophet Isaiah says he never shirked his duty, never turned back. Men beat him, buffeted him, pulled at his beard and he did not so much as shield his face. That was how sure he was that his help was in the LORD.

The second reading is an early Christian hymn. It tells how the story of the passion ended for those who believe in Christ. His humanness was real, not a sham. Consequently he faced death when it came in the ordinary way of a man who cannot do anything about it. What came of this was exaltation and reverence — even divine honors. The one who emptied himself was filled. His name became the highest name. Jesus is Lord.

The Marcan passion contains the same dreary account you might find on any police blotter or jailer's files if they bothered to record these things. Someone is picked up, questioned. Hearsay evidence is dealt with as if it made a real charge. Nothing is uncovered so Jesus is scourged on principle. The soldiers are bored stiff in this outpost of empire far from their homes in Britain, Africa and Greece. They hear that the prisoner thinks he is a king. To Pilate this religious claim has serious civil overtones but the soldiers find it merely amusing. They have a mad Jew on their hands and they treat him accordingly.

The story of Jesus' passion is the story of our times. There is ignorance and frustration everywhere: men trapped in ghettoes, in armies, in foreign wars, in political systems they cannot respect. Power stands aloof making money from the conflict, from the miseries of the poor. The newspaper last Monday had a long and powerful article about the plight of the Indians who cut rubber in upper Argentina along the Amazon River, totally illiterate, broken men at forty. One plantation owner said the trouble was they had Mass only once a year and he was going to try to get it for them once a month. What a blasphemy! To celebrate the body of Christ in the midst of those boken bodies who *are* the body of Christ.

Or take the current war. Three weeks ago I spent an afternoon at McGuire Air Force Base giving testimony at the hearing of a captain who is trying to resign his commission. I was being asked what the Catholic Church taught on peace and war. Captain Franci, the man in question, is a Viet Nam veteran who flies the big ones, bombers and transport planes. He said he never in twenty-four months heard anyone in the U.S. forces call a Vietnamese a Vietnamese. The people of the north were always Charlie or the Cong, the people of the south, presumably our allies, were always "zips." He said he shortly came to realize that killing was an endurable business so long as you were able to classify these people as somehow subhuman, a breed less than yourself, totally different in their needs and desires. You can kill a population you can think of as zips. You would lose your mind if you began to think of them as people like yourself.

The police in every country in the world, like the soldiers in Jesus' time, are having a terrible time understanding why good people should be opposed to war or racism. The clergy and sisters and brothers, the intellectuals fare badly at the hands of police whether in Brazil or here. Our police and FBI are outraged, totally undone, when they see supposed upholders of law and order — the supreme examples of shaping up, toeing the mark — walking on picket lines, going limp, disturbing the draft system, going to jail. They react just as the soldiery in the passion narrative did: by acts of brutality against something they cannot understand. Black kids they can cope with. They think up names for them, like zips. That way they can deal with them as something less than human. But this other crowd, who ought to know better than to go against the law, what can you do with them? The religious types represent the disintegration of the universe, the way these simple, narrow people have it figured out. All the custodians of the law can do is smash brutally at this new world of silent innocence.

What Jesus does for us is remind us what it is to be human. And a world of inhumanity can have nothing to do with any policy so mad as that.

March 22, 1970   Our Lady of Mercy Parish

THE PASCHAL TRIDUUM

HOLY THURSDAY
Ex 12:1-8, 11-14; 1 Cor 11:23-26; Jn 13:1-15

Today commemorates a meal and an act of service. I mean, of course, the institution of the eucharist and Jesus' washing of his disciples' feet. There is a third liturgical observance in our Roman Church, the center of Catholicity for the West and a portion of the East. I refer to the so-called "chrism Mass" in cathedral churches. It is celebrated in the forenoon by the bishop and his presbyters.

The oils of catechumens, of confirmands, and of the sick are blessed for distribution to all the churches and chapels in a diocese where those rites are celebrated. Lately it has been given a special clerical cast by the non-historical invitation to priests to renew their commitment in that office. The theory may be that not many laity attend anyway but this is a way to ensure it.

There is still a fourth observance connected with this day. It dates to medieval times and some of you with European backgrounds will know about it. It is the entombment of Christ in image, along with his sacramental reservation until tomorrow's communion service. The practice lies at the heart of the Forty Hours Devotion which emerged from it in sixteenth-century Italy. The custom seems to have begun in the Teutonic north as early as the tenth century, when we have a record of Forty Hours Prayer in the vicinity of a simulated tomb. A crucifix at first and later a carving of the dead body of Jesus was reposed in a specified place for veneration — sometimes with the eucharistic body placed alongside it, often without. Right up to the present the place where the Sacrament is kept is called in liturgical language *locus repositionis* and *repositorium* but also *sepulchrum*. We have a record going back to the 1200s of a town in Italy called Zara which began its "supplication of the forty hours" on the evening of today's feast *in Coena Domini*, "the Lord's Supper." Putting the conclusion of the liturgy at 8:00 PM, you have a four-hour period Thursday night, twenty-four on Friday, and twelve on Saturday, which brings you to the Gloria of the Easter Mass at midnight. In medieval Hereford and Rouen the cross only was placed in the sepulcher but in Salisbury the Blessed Sacrament also. It is this more austere tradition that has survived in the Roman Rite, with its reservation of the holy bread in a chalice (to stand for a tomb) and its veneration of the cross tomorrow separated from one another. But take comfort, all you of the Lithuanian and Czech and Slovak and Hispanic nations for whom Holy Week is nothing without the life-sized figure of the dead Christ. The custom is a thousand years old and the Roman See always deals with it respectfully as if it were a part of liturgy even though it did not get into our liturgical books.

I have spoken of the eucharistic meal up till now only obliquely. In part that is because this day is not an observance of that mystery only. In 1951 Pope Pius XII restored the ancient *lotio pedum* or footwashing into the Roman Rite on an experimental basis. In 1955 it became obligatory. As you doubtless know from a lively childhood memory, the Holy Week rites were the least revised after Vatican II because the work had been so thoroughly done fifteen years before. What we now have and are experiencing this evening is a veneration of the Lord's body in his holy Sacrament and a veneration of that same body in the sister and the brother. The reminder is a salutary one. What would it profit us to eat and drink him sacramentally if we despised any human being he died to save? A church with separate sections for blacks and whites at Mass is an abomination. Does the very notion shock you? It was still a lively custom when I went to Washington, D.C., in 1943. The Church of the Blessed Sacrament on Broad Street where Fairmount and Ridge meet, for five years now the Greater Exodus Baptist Church, was built by Mother Drexel's private fortune because black Catholics were not welcome in St. Malachy or St. Elizabeth or St. Mary of the Assumption or Our Lady of Mercy. They made handsome silver monstrances and lunulas and pyxes for the body of Christ in sixteenth-century Mexico and Ecuador and Peru, while his body was being crucified by the *conquistadores* in the Indians who mined the silver.

At present in the church which we ourselves are women may not be priests, priests of the West may not marry, layfolk in the absence of a priest may not have the eucharistic Christ, the spread of the gospel is confined to the spread of the clergy, all because Jesus in his lifetime is said to have decreed it so. Or have various classes of oppressors to three of which I belong — white Western, male, presbyter — decreed it so? There may not be a uniquely Tamil or Ibo Mass rite for the reason that the Europeans in control do not trust the Asian, the African spirit in prayer.

A Swiss Capuchin friar named Walbert Bühlmann, a professor of missions now in Rome helping in the government of his order, wrote a book recently called *The Coming of the Third Church*. Visiting in this country this spring, he has been telling in his mild and gentle way how the Congregation for the Teaching of Faith tried to have his book recalled for its errors in Catholic faith. Of course there are none. He is a loyal son of the church who happens to see, as any thoughtful person can, the shape of the twenty-first century. The Catholics of the third and fourth worlds — Latin America, Africa, to a lesser degree Asia and Oceania — will simply outnumber the Catholics of Europe and its dutiful child North America. And then the liberated will liberate. Not from all restraints. Not from the *askēsis*, the discipline of the gospel. But from those cultural shackles whereby Christ in the eucharistic rite is made the chief jailer, not God's chosen one as the chief setter-free.

Pope John Paul wrote a remarkable encyclical letter, his first, dated March 4 this year. Its chief message is ethical. It has to do with human freedom. Let me read two paragraphs from its central portion:

> The situation of humanity in the modern world represents, so to say, the gigantic development of the parable in the Bible of the rich banqueter and the poor man Lazarus. So widespread is the phenomenon that it brings into question the financial, monetary, production and commercial mechanisms that, resting on various political pressures, support the world economy. These are proving incapable either of remedying the unjust social situations inherited from the past or of dealing with the urgent challenges and ethical demands of the present. By submitting humanity to tensions created by itself, depleting at an accelerated pace material and energy resources, and compromising the geophysical environment, these structures unceasingly make the areas of misery spread, accompanied by anguish, frustration and bitterness.
>
> We have before us here a great drama that can leave no one indifferent. The person who, on the one hand, is trying to draw the maximum profit and, on the other hand, is paying the price

in damage and injury is always the human creature. The drama is made still worse by the presence close at hand of the privileged social classes and of the rich countries which accumulate goods to an excessive degree, and the misuse of those riches is very often the cause of various ills. Add to this the fever of inflation and the plague of unemployment and you have further symptoms of the moral disorder that is observable everywhere in the world situation. The situation therefore requires daring creative resolves in keeping with authentic human dignity.

The Pope is calling for the reform of every global social institution, a courageous venture. Yet he seems to go on the assumption that the social institution that is the church and the social institutions within the church do not themselves need reform. But he is young and he is keen and in God's providence he has time to learn.

We are not here to examine the Pope's situation tonight. We are here to examine our own.

As we eat the Lord's body and drink his blood yet another time we resolve that it will never serve as an instrument of oppression for us but always liberation: from our baser passions, from our prejudices, from the will to dominate and control, from the desire to down another person, another people, another faith.

Jesus is the freest of human beings. No tomb can hold him because sin has no grip on him. As it is with him let it be with us. That is the Eucharist's only meaning, for he — and we —are *corpus Domini Jesu Christi*, the body of Jesus Christ who is Lord.

April 12, 1979   Temple University Newman Center

GOOD FRIDAY

Is 52:13—53:12; Heb 4:14-16; 5:7-9; Jn 18:1—19:42

A tall, shy-looking teenager climbs on a bus, pays his fare and makes his way to a back seat, clutching something under his arm. No one in the bus pays much attention to him at first but within minutes everyone is conscious of his presence. Loud, blaring rock music comes from the transistor radio he now has next to his ear. He is smiling to himself, totally unaware of the effect his sound system is having on the other passengers.

The scene could be anywhere in city or country. Countless studies have been done and articles written as to the *why* of this phenomenon. Why do young people have a compelling need for this constant presence? Why the piercing loudness? Is it a form of escape? If so, escape from what? I had lunch today at The Meeting House across the street with a Temple secretary, the mother of two teenagers. The jukebox was going pretty strongly I thought. She said she found it a great relief from home. Will this same craving for noise exist in the next generation? No one is really sure. One guess is as good as another. Perhaps those of us who complain the most about this characteristic among young people have devised our own ways of shutting out the silence — the awful, awful silence.

We do not know what to do with the gift of silence in today's screeching, noise-filled world. Our senses are being bombarded constantly, not only by the commerical media but by everyone around us. There is almost a compulsion to fill the void of silence with sound. We let it go on because we are afraid of what might happen if the music stopped, even for a few hours. We have turned silence, an old, old friend, into a stranger who cannot be trusted, even an enemy who must be destroyed. Lately one of our graduate students in religion, a woman, returned from a six-months' stay in Tübingen, a sleepy country town in Germany which has a large university and lots of cows. She boarded with a widow and went to the library daily. Coming home she said she had trouble enduring the stereo set in the apartment upstairs — something she never noticed before.

We treasure our powers of communication, our ability to converse, to teach, to encourage, to protest. Our powers of speech are not simply part of us, they are us. They are the way we are known and understood. What term, in fact, do we use to say that God makes himself known to people? None other than "the word," or "God speaks to us." That simple and all-inclusive term "the word" says everything about God present to humanity in the person of Jesus. In tonight's liturgy, however, the Word expresses himself in wordlessness. He lets the power of silence exert itself in all its fullness. The Jesus we meet in today's readings is the silent Jesus, silent first under torture and finally silenced by death. "Though he was harshly treated," prophesies Isaiah, "he submitted and opened not his mouth; like a lamb led to the slaughter or a sheep before the shearers he was silent and opened not his mouth." The few words recorded by St. John during the course of his inquiry before Annas are restrained, almost dispassionate. "I have spoken publicly to any who would listen," he says. "Why do you question me? Question those who heard me when I spoke . . . they will know what I said." And then later, before Pilate: "Anyone committed to the truth hears my voice" (v. 37). A few phrases on the cross and, finally: "Now it is finished." Before, there had been in his life a time for teaching, persuading, moving hearts through the spoken word. Now there is a time for silence, for letting the motions of giving himself over totally speak for themselves — with an intensity of sound greater than any that his spoken words could produce.

If the event represented by the death of Jesus is ever to touch us, we must let something happen to us. We can offer ourselves to our brothers and sisters as Jesus offered himself to us only if we are in full possession of ourselves. Our offering must be whole and human if it is to be of any use to them. The needed quality goes by any number of names: wisdom, holiness, maturity. It is learned in the classroom called life. Often the young possess it; some who are old never do. Friendship with silence, the most skillful of teachers, is very much a part of this growth. Silence lets us ponder what God is doing in our lives and grasp whatever truth lies in human words and events. It gives us back to ourselves; it puts the broken bits and pieces together again.

There is a silence that is cowardly, like the silence of Christians in Germany when Hitler was destroying Jews by the millions, like the silence of white Americans in the face of the killing off of their black brothers, like the silence of citizens in the face of war crimes of their government — the attempted destruction of a whole nation in the name of freedom. No one can praise this silence. It is the voice of death and hell.

Jesus protested the evil that was being done against him —in the garden, in his trial before Pilate, with a loud cry from the cross. But he spoke with a silence that was louder still. His was the silence of suffering love which made it possible to be a slave; to be imprisoned and never brought to trial; to be a Soledad brother; to go to jail for trying to awaken a national conscience. The silence of Jesus forces us to think of all the evils we support with our ready talk.

April 9, 1971   Our Lady of Mercy Parish

An Ecumenical Service,
The Seven Last Words of Christ,
St. Asaph's Episcopal Church,
Bala Cynwyd, Pennsylvania
Good Friday, April 13, 1979

GOOD FRIDAY 1979

Homilies on the Seven Last Words of Christ
Lk 23:34, 43; Jn 19:26, 27; Mk 15:34 (Mt 27:46); Jn 19:28; Lk 23:46; Jn 19:30

I. "Father, forgive them for they know not what they do." Lk 23:34.

St. Luke likes to record snatches of the prayer life of Jesus as his means of underscoring his humanity. So we are not surprised to find this word of Jesus from the cross addressed to God, chronologically the first, in Luke alone. It occurs in the midst of the laconic statement of Mk and Mt, "And they crucified him [then the Lucan insertion] dividing his garments among them by casting lots." Luke's Jesus is a figure of forgiveness at all points. We are not surprised that he should be one at the last. Peter will say to the Jerusalem crowd at the Beautiful Gate in the book of Acts — remember, this too is Luke's composition — "Yet I know, my brothers, that you acted out of ignorance, just as your leaders did" (3:17). Stephen forgives those who stone him just before he dies (Ac 7:60).

The legal axiom says: "Ignorance is no excuse." We are expected to apprise ourselves of our responsibilities. We cannot go blissfully uninformed and expect to be blameless. Is it so different with God than with us humans? The question is not a fair one because a very different thing is going on in the gospels than mere blame-fixing for Jesus' death. The evangelist, in a sense, could not be less interested than he is in the cruelty of the executioners, the complicity of Pilate and the priestly leadership, the fickleness of the crowd. His great concern is that we have Jesus straight, not the lesser players in the drama. "Father, forgive them." When Jesus is removed from the earthly scene, he is for Luke "the Lord" in glory, the heavenly intercessor for our needs. The church is a community reconciled by virtue of Jesus' power with the Father and his gift of the Spirit.

A bumper sticker can be seen these days that says: "Christians aren't better than other people. Just forgiven." That's pretty repulsive, despite its earnest theological intent. Whoever composed it knows the gospel message of forgiveness, but is constrained to confine its effects to persons with a certain kind of faith — his own. Luckily for us, it is to be hoped, God is not so confined. He is so powerful that he can forgive even Christians of the bumper-sticker kind — or your kind or mine. The very heart of his deed in Christ is forgiveness. The whole human race is a people reconciled.

Must we know about it to profit by it? Accept it to live in the new state of forgiveness? We cannot escape the problem of knowledge versus ignorance. Are the ignorant forgiven along with the rest? Are only those ignorant of their guilt forgiven? Must we try to make our way out of darkness if God is to forgive us at all?

In the poem of a contemporary Pole, a worker in an armaments factory says:

> I only turn screws, weld together
>   parts of destruction,
> never grasping the whole, or the human lot.
> I could do otherwise (would parts be left out?) . . . .
> Though what I create is all wrong,
>   the world's evil is none of my doing.
> But is that enough?

God forgives us.
He does not answer all our questions.

II. "Today thou shalt be with me in Paradise." Lk 23:43.

As with the first word of Jesus from the cross, so the second comes to us from Luke only. The brigands from a recent zealot uprising who flank him merely revile him in Mark and Matthew. In Luke one rails at him, the other defends him. Jesus has done nothing wrong, this one says, while they die justly. The theme of Jesus' innocence is tied in Luke-Acts to the innocence of the Christians vis-à-vis the Jews and Romans. A messiah crucified as a malefactor was a great problem for the early church. He was not out to disturb institutions or subvert public order any more than his followers were. Yet that seemed to be what happened whenever his teaching was taken seriously. It is a problem that has not managed to go away.

"Today you will be with me in Paradise," says Jesus. The criminal has said, in good Jewish expectation of the final age: "Jesus, remember me when you come in your kingly power." To this Jesus replies: "Truly, I say to you, this day you shall be with me in Paradise." He substitutes the prospect of being with him at the death of both for the deferred hope of a future rule of God. Something has happened to the Jewish idea of the messianic age in Christian circles by the time Luke writes his gospel. He has done a similar thing in Jesus' parable of the rich man and the beggar, again a story which he alone tells. In it, Lazarus at death is carried by angels to the bosom of Abraham while the rich man is in torment in the abode of the dead. Both are experiencing the fruits of their conduct now, not in some distant execution of judgment. Yet Luke maintains the Jewish hope of a glorious son of man who will act as God's judge: "But when the son of man comes, will he find any faith on the earth?" Which is it to be? Will the dead go or the son of man come?

There are great problems in the Christian belief in divine retribution. We love to anticipate God's judgment, certain that the justice can be no less than ours but secretly doubting it. He shows such poor judgment in the short run that we wonder how he can be trusted in the long.

Death, judgment, the resurrection of the dead, heaven, hell. It is all too much for us. We decide not to break our heads over it. And then a loved one dies, a close acquaintance, or it is we ourselves who feel twinges of mortality. "This day thou shalt be with me in Paradise." Who heard that word? The one who asked to be remembered. The one without illusions who could tell the just from the unjust, the innocent Jesus from his guilty self.

Our age is sick over guilt. It is laden with it, drowns in it. Yet it knows next to nothing of sin. If it could acknowledge sin it might be rid of guilt.

We look for Paradise here. It eludes us and we say it is nowhere. But it is where the obedient Jesus is; this day. We need not die to taste it. We need only acknowledge that we pay the price for what we have done. There is one, only one, who has done nothing wrong. To know the justice of the just one is already to enter with him on his reign.

III. "Woman, behold thy son." "Son, behold thy mother." Jn 19:26, 27

Jesus' mother is a mysterious figure in all four gospels. The evangelist John does not even provide her name. It can be argued from the gospels that she is the first believer in her son — as is done from the Cana story: "Do whatever he tells you" — or that she shares the skepticism of his other kinsmen who, lumped together as "his family," say: "He is out of his senses" (Mk 3:21). The safest thing to say is that none of the four gospels informs us on Mary's state of mind or heart. They all use her to further their theological purposes. Thus, in a famous word attributed to Jesus, "Those who hear the word of God and keep it" are declared blessed rather than she whose womb bore him and whose breasts nursed him. But that is not a saying about Mary, it is a saying about fidelity.

The same kind of thing is going on in Jesus' third word from the cross spoken to his mother. Of importance is the first part of the verse: "Seeing his mother there with the disciple whom he loved, Jesus said . . ." and so on. The center of gravity in the exchange proves to be that disciple, "who took her into his care." He is the chief apostolic authority for the author of John's gospel. We are sure of that.

Who, then, is Mary? She is the "woman" addressed by Jesus in his first sign, when his hour is not yet come (2:4), become the "woman" of his last sign. "Father, the hour has come. Give glory to your son" (17:1). "From that hour onward," the hour in which his glory was revealed, she was committed to the company of a beloved friend.

The woman of the Bible best known as simply "the woman" is Eve. Her name means "life" for she is the mother of all living. But Jesus' gift in the fourth gospel is life. All who come to him have life. He is entrusting the woman who authored his life to the community that has life in him. It is not straining hard to see in her the mother of the church. Indeed, St. Justin Martyr not many years later followed him in the imagery as did St. Irenaeus shortly after that. If Jesus is the new Adam, then she who is so closely associated with him in his life-giving work is the new Eve. The suggestion is that these perceptive two did not impose the imagery on the fourth gospel but derived it from that gospel. You and I, beloved offspring of God, have the church as our mother. But the mother of the church is a particular woman. Her son and our brother Jesus gave her to us.

The oldest charge that women can lay at the door of men is that they use them, manipulate them, deal with them in thorough ambivalence. I think the charge is true. It is further said that in the community called church men have devised endless stratagems clothed in the language of the sacred to keep women down, control them. I think the charge is true. Has Jesus any part in that pious scheme? None whatever. He gave us Mary to keep us free and we have used her as a symbol of bondage.

Who needs a mother like that?

IV. "My God, my God, why hast thou forsaken me?" Mk 15:34; Mt 27:46

The ninth hour is three in the afternoon in a world that reckons the beginning of the day at six. It is the time, Mark and Matthew tell us, when Jesus uttered his cry of dereliction from the cross. This outcry is a stumbling-block to Christians. Even Luke when he comes on it in Mark omits it and has Jesus commend his spirit to his Father (23:46). The phrase comes from Psalm 22; it is, indeed, its opening line. Pedants like to point out that by the time you reach verse 30 the psalmist is saying: "To him my soul shall live;/ my descendants shall serve him./ Let the coming generation be told of the LORD ...[and] the justice he has shown." Jesus would have recited this psalm through to the end, say these earnest apologists. Therefore we have a canticle of hope, not of despair.

I think the theory has nothing to be said in its favor. The reason is that the bulk of the psalm is the heart's cry of a suffering Jew which supplied all sorts of phrases to the passion narratives. "In you our fathers trusted, and you delivered them . . . . All who see me scoff at me; they mock me with parted lips, they wag their heads: He relied on the Lord; let him deliver him, let him rescue him if he loves him . . . . They have pierced my hands and my feet. They have numbered all my bones . . . . They divide my vesture among them, and for my vesture they cast lots."

No, it is a cry of dereliction, all right; not despair that gives up hope, but utter dismay that does not know what to make of the life of trust. Jesus has not forsaken God. But every appearance is that God has forsaken him. The Christian, the Jew, has been in that place many times since. Where is God? It is not that his presence is not felt, it is that God seems to have actively abandoned the ones who try to serve him.

Comforter, where, where, is your comforting? . . .
My cries heave, herds-long; huddle in a main, a chief-
woe, world-sorrow; on an age-old anvil wince and sin —

Then lull, then leave off. . . .
O the mind, mind has mountains; cliffs of fall
Frightful, sheer, no-man-fathomed. Hold them cheap
May who ne'er hung there. . . .

Jesus on the cross knows something of those mountains of the mind, those cliffs of fall. He is a real savior to those who have lost contact with what people call "reality." Like them, he has made contact with nothingness, the abyss.

And he has come back. I do not mean from death, for the people I speak of have looked forward to inviting death. He has come back from God-forsakenness to God-enfoldedness. He knew what to make of death just before he went out to meet it.

V. "I thirst." Jn 19:28

Once Jesus had turned his mother over to the care of the disciple whom he loved he realized, says John, that everything was now finished. By that the evangelist does not mean over and done with but perfected, completed. There remains an incompleteness, though, a sense of something undone. To mark it, Jesus said from the cross in order to fulfill the Scripture, "I thirst." Undoubtedly John has in mind here the verse of the psalm which says: "My throat is dried up like baked clay,/ my tongue cleaves to my jaws" (22:15). In the gospel, a sponge is affixed to a rod of hyssop and Jesus' thirst is slaked by a taste of wine. It is called *oxos*, common wine, the soldier's daily ration of rotgut. The reference, again, is biblical: "They put gall in my food,/ and in my thirst they gave me vinegar to drink" (Ps 69:21).

The evangelist John never simply means what he says but always more. Matthew quotes fulfillment texts by the score and that is what he means by them: in this word or deed of

Jesus this ancient text is fulfilled. With John there are always echoes of echoes of echoes.

> Whoever drinks this water will thirst again,
> But whoever drinks the water I give will never thirst;
> the water I give shall become a fountain within,
>   leaping up unto eternal life (4:14)

and

> No one who believes in me shall ever thirst (6:35)

and

> If anyone thirst let him come to me;
> Let the one who believes in me drink.
> Scripture says: From within that one, rivers of
>   living water shall flow (7:37; cf. Is 12:3).

Of old the prophet said of the final days:

> The channels of Judah shall flow with water:
> A fountain shall gush from the house of the LORD (Joel 4:18)

But Jesus is that temple from which the fountain shall flow: "Destroy this temple and in three days I will raise it up." The edifice is crumbling. Its dissolution is at hand. To be sure of it, "One of the soldiers thrust a lance into his side and immediately blood — and water — flowed out" (19:34).

The slaker of every thirst is himself athirst. But the water has begun to flow as Ezekiel promised: "I saw water flowing out from beneath the threshold of the temple toward the east . . . a river through which I could not wade. . . . Along both banks of the river, fruit trees of every kind shall grow; their leaves shall not fail nor their fruit fail."

Long ago an English mystic wrote: "I saw in Christ a double thirst: one bodily, another ghostly . . . . Methought the drying of Christ's flesh was the greatest pain of the Passion, and the last . . . . As for the ghostly thirst . . . when He was in pain, we were in pain . . . and all creatures who knew him not had this for their pain, that all creatures, sun and moon, withdrew their service, and so were left in sorrow for the time."

He thirsts when we serve him not. We thirst when we serve him not. "For I know well that he who bought me at so sore cost would release me when he willed."

VI. "Father, into thy hands I commend my spirit." Lk 23:46

In the Roman office at Compline — the Evensong of the Book of Common Prayer — the sixth word of Jesus from the cross is sung to a haunting melody. Let me try it, choir monk that I have never been: *"In manus tuas, Domine, commendo spiritum meum."* "Into thy hands, O Lord, I commend my spirit." A medieval English night-prayer would later translate that: "I pray the Lord my soul to keep." The 31st Psalm from which Luke takes it has been saying things like: "You are my rock of refuge, my stronghold" and "O LORD, let me not be put to shame, for I call on you." The whole psalm is, quite simply, a commendation of one's fate and lot, one's whole person, to the God of Israel. Verse 6 in the Greek speaks of committing one's spirit, meaning one's whole self, over to God. The phrase is ready-made for Luke who will declare that, upon saying this, Jesus breathed forth his spirit. He does not mean anything as simple as expired in the sense of died. He intends to say, along with Mark whom he follows and Matthew who is even more explicit, that with a loud cry Jesus yielded the spirit over.

The life-breath of Jesus is given back to God, God who first breathed into Adam's nostrils to make him a living being. Not only, however, does Jesus return his life-breath to God. He sends it out upon his disciples much as he later breathed on them the breath of Holy Spirit in the upper room (Jn 20:22). The movement is twofold: toward God and toward us.

We probably would not be able to say this if it were not so clear from the rest of Luke-Acts that Jesus' gift to the infant church is the gift of the spirit. While in death he is safe in God's hands, so in risen life he commends us as much as himself to God. We are a people to whom the very spirit of God has been transmitted, therefore who live and breathe by his breath.

The evangelists, you will notice, do not tarry over Jesus' psychological states, his inmost thoughts and feelings. They know that a just man has died unjustly, that there is in Jesus' death a paradigm of the innocent sufferer. But that is not an area of major concern for them. The spirit of medieval passion piety which flourishes even until now would elude them, I think. So conscious are they of the cosmic drama that is being played out on the cross that they turn to the sacred page to express what is happening on Calvary. That knob of sandstone, Calvary, is the meeting-place of heaven and earth for them, literally the navel of the world.

As Jesus dies so does all just humanity die. We have no idea how we will face death: in sleep, violently on a highway, surrounded by family, alone. All we know is that the spirit of God has been committed to us. In life, in death, we must hand it over.

VII. "It is finished." Jn 19:30

This final word of Jesus from the cross is given us by John. It comes immediately after his declaration of thirst and the mention of the sour wine put to his lips. "When Jesus took the wine, he said, 'It is finished.' Then he bowed his head and delivered over the spirit." The passion narrative in John, it seems, has as its goal not to awaken the reader's sympathies for Jesus but to celebrate a victory. Jesus, the victor, followed the unswerving cause of the love of God to his last breath.

St. John presents Jesus' suffering and death as part of his exaltation and glory. Jesus is in complete charge as Lord before the high priest. His answer to him reveals him as the final judge of the world. The exchange with Pilate is the occasion for declarations about the world's unbelief. Jesus' last words from the cross, "It is finished," means perfected, completed, and is a statement of victory. Nothing in the passion and death happens against his will. All is an act of free obedience to the Father. And now it is done. The work is over. Jesus goes back to God, goes to the place above where he was before. To be sure, the fourth evangelist knows the players in the passion story as well as the next one: the disciples, Mary, the one whom Jesus loved, his mother. Yet he employs them differently from the others, namely to highlight Jesus' lordly behavior.

It is not easy for us to contemplate the death of Christ on the cross like the evangelists of old time. They, like him, are first-century Jews soaked in the Scriptures, seeing everything written there as fulfilled in him. We do not think as they do. At times it is not easy to be nourished by them. There was a woman who lived in England six centuries ago whom we recognize as a modern person, our style. I mean Juliana of

Norwich who recorded her visions of Jesus suffering as *The Showing of God's Love*. She wrote:

> This has ever been a comfort to me: that I chose Jesus for my heaven in all this time of passion and sorrow, and it has been a learning to me, that I should evermore do so, and choose only him for my heaven in weal and in woe.
>
> Thus saw I my Lord Jesus languishing for a long time, for the oneing of the Godhead, for love, gave him strength to suffer more than all might suffer. I mean not alone more pain than all might suffer, but also that he suffered more anguish than all that ever were, from the first beginning to the last day . . . . For he who was highest and worthiest was most completely despoiled and most utterly humiliated. But the love that made Him suffer all this — it passes as far all his pains as heaven is above earth. For the passion was a deed done in time by the working of love; but the love is without beginning, and is, and ever shall be, without any end. (Ch. XI)

As Juliana beholds the cross, Jesus upon it changes to a blissful expression of countenance. This changing of his expression made her change hers. And she thought: " 'Where is now any point at thy pain or of thy grief?' And I was full merry." Merry? At the cross? She means it literally. "What, do you wish to know our Lord's meaning in this thing? Know it well. Love was his meaning . . . . Who reveals it to you? Love. What did he reveal to you? Love. Why does he reveal it to you? For love.."

EASTER SUNDAY
Ac 10:34a, 37-43; 1 Cor 5:6-8; Jn 20:1-9

The Christians of the East celebrate the feast of the Resurrection next Sunday. That is because a canon of the Council of Nicaea in 325 decreed that it should be observed on the Sunday after the Jewish Passover. But Passover is not a matter of a single day, rather of a whole week. Listen to the way things are prescribed in Exodus 13:

> For seven days you shall eat unleavened bread [in Hebrew, *matzoth*] and the seventh day shall also be a festival to the LORD. Only unleavened bread may be eaten during the seven days; no leaven and nothing leavened may be found in all your territory (vv. 6-7).

The Christian West, perhaps oblivious of the week-long character of Pesach, legislated differently; it reckoned Easter as the first Sunday after the first full moon after the vernal or spring equinox. There was the paschal full moon last Wednesday night, all right, but in the West we do not wait for the seven days of *matzoth* to elapse. This constituted a painful East-West difference in the early days. It is one of the reasons the East considers the West unorthodox: that we of the West have departed from a strict interpretation of Nicaea.

St. Paul may have been writing his first letter to his Corinthian converts in the spring of the year. If so, this would account for his use of the figure of the bit of yeast that is corrupting them. The immediate context in the epistle is their tolerance of incest in the community — a man living with his father's wife (v. 1). Their arrogance, in Paul's eyes, consists in their supposition that they can "handle it." It was, after all, Corinth, which had provided the Greek language with the word "to corinthize," i.e., to engage in sexual debauchery.

The old yeast of corruption and wickedness need not be sexual, obviously. Reading the sickening stories of human slaughter in Idi Amin's Kampala is instructive. In a basement under the security headquarters prospective victims had to remove the last corpse from a gutter to a nearby pile before becoming the next victim. The stench of the dead pervades the place where liberators are still discovering the living. Some of them are in an emaciated condition from having been there three and four weeks and survived on the flesh of others. It sounds like the death camps of Hitler days. We have in Philadelphia, where I live, a black high school principal who, as a GI, was part of the liberating force at Buchenwald. He is very active in the business of educating Americans, black and white, to the genocidal possibilities that lurk in the human heart.

When St. Paul urges believers in Jesus as the risen Christ to be rid of the old yeast of corruption and wickedness he is speaking to all believers down the ages. For, indeed, it is our faith that in this man whom God raised from the dead, his only son, we have life. Yet our tendency in every age is to choose death, to go the downward path that corrupts the human image and degrades it in ourselves and in others.

Yesterday's paper told of a parish in a deteriorated section of Jersey City where the people made the way of the cross by stopping at fourteen scenes of violent crime: muggings, rapes, the beating to death of an 86-year-old woman in her home. The Pope, new in Rome, expresses surprise that he cannot go in safety without a heavy police guard from one place to another in that city. Ten-year-old boys in this country know what blocks in their neighborhood they cannot walk on for fear of rival gangs.

In the midst of all this the consumption of goods and services rises among the rich and the very comfortable in ways that you and I can scarcely envision. The plea continues to be made on humanitarian grounds for abortions for the poor. This is not because the poor are especially opposed to life —often they are its best supporters — but because they are at the bottom of a social scheme marked by immense injustices. The idea of getting at causes rather than at symptoms like abortion occurs to some. But the injustices are of such long standing and go so deep that a kind of helplessness overtakes the whole culture, pro- and anti-abortion forces alike. It is easier to get wrought up over symptoms. Attending to causes is too much a matter of purging out the old yeast of corruption and wickedness. It would require radical attention to the national outlook on money and sex and power and race. We are so busy at the game of consumerism, along with shouting "praise Jesus," that we have not much time for that.

The Easter feast is a sobering one no matter how it is viewed. It gives immense comfort to millions because it announces that death is not the end. For them — I trust that means for us — it is a season of hope. Sin and death are realities in our lives. We recognize in Jesus their conqueror.

Yet the victory appears tenuous because the presence of evil and the fact of death are so pervasive. We wonder, at times, if we play out a charade in celebrating the mysteries of Christianity. The realities of war and world hunger and indeed our own mortality seem such powerful evidence against the Easter hope. Are we not just whistling in the dark?

There is a sign of hope arising from a new quarter, so vast are the possibilities of godhead. That sign is the continuing incarnation of God in what are called the "young peoples" of the globe, chiefly in the southern hemisphere. While western countries and Japan are preoccupied with the problems of old age, forty-three percent of the populations in Asia and South America are under fifteen years of age. Two-thirds of the population of the two continents is under twenty-five. That means from a Christian perspective — surely not the only one — that the churches of the south, like its peoples, are churches of youth.

That statistic does not fill everyone with hope. It chills the hearts of many with its possibilities of chaos. Who will run the international conglomerates? Does that not spell the end of the technical know-how to feed those populations? Will the globe not destroy itself with the six billion or so projected for the year 2000 at present rates of population growth? A world run by young people? Who can endure the thought?

The God who is the Father of all can endure the thought. The one who saved the world by a man in his thirties, from the "third world" of his time, can endure the thought. For Jesus' reliance on God was greater than the force of sin or death or evil in high places.

April 15, 1979   St. Stephen Martyr Parish

EASTER SUNDAY
Ac 10:34, 37-43; Col 3:1-4; Jn 20:1-9

In a poem called *Spring*, the English Catholic poet Hopkins asks:

What is all this juice and all this joy?
A strain of the earth's sweet being in the beginning
In Eden garden. . . .

Well, it may be such a strain of being but this spring has taught us that its juice is likely to be connected with a falling barometer. The joy is an easier matter. It is that Christ is risen. "He is truly risen as he said, Alleluia!"

Break the box and shed the nard;
Stop not now to count the cost;
Hither bring the pearl, opal, sard;
Reck not what the poor have lost,
Upon Christ throw all away:
Know ye, this is Easter Day.

(Hopkins, *Easter*)

The gospels are at some pains to tell us that no one saw Jesus coming forth from the tomb. All of the reports are about an accomplished fact, whether deduced from an empty sepulcher or made known by Jesus' appearance to the women, to the travelers to Emmaus, to his disciples. The whole point of the resurrection accounts is that death and life have been in contest and that life has won. Jesus is not the king of the dead. He is the king of life.

Throughout the New Testament, faith in Christ is closely identified with life. That is important to remember, for popular versions of it have made it one large abstention from life's joys, a drawn out Mass of Requiem. But Christian faith is life in Christ with emphasis on the life. If a thing is not life then it is not Christ.

An old joke has a man asking: "Doc, if I stay away from cigarettes and liquor, from fast women and slow horses, will I live to be a hundred?" And the doctor says: "No, it'll just seem that way."

I am not trying to enlist Christ on the side of self-indulgence or the sporting life. I *am* enlisting him on the side of life, for the gospel puts him nowhere else.

"Jesus of Nazareth, the one who was crucified, is risen . . ." (Mk 16:6).

"Touch me and see; no ghost has flesh and bones as you can see that I have . . ." (Lk 24:39). "Mary Magdalene went to the disciples. 'I have seen the Lord,' she said" (Jn 20:18). . . . " 'You know neither the Scriptures nor the power of God,' said Jesus . . . . 'He is not the God of the dead but of the living' " (Mt 22:29, 32).

By "life," the gospel means what it says — human existence without limitation. We have done something strange with this conviction and have concluded — wrongly — that if we can manage not to live it to the full now we will later. Half life, shadow life, imitation life here; full life, real life, eternal life hereafter.

The gospel word we translate "eternal" means "pertaining to the final age, authentic, total." It does not mean "endless," least of all "what begins after death." The ancient Egyptians were experts in life after death. The Greeks treasured immortality — *athanasiá*, they called it. The risen life of Jesus is something different. It is the Jewish hope spoken of in the book of Daniel — that in the God of Israel, "many who sleep in the dust of the earth shall awake." It is more. The chief meaning of Jesus' victory over death — at least in John — is not that life begins when we die. Life begins when we admit God's will into our lives as Jesus did. What will follow from a life so lived, God knows. That, in a strict sense, is God's business. He will go on conquering death when we die in a way known to him, the same God who has conquered death in us during life. The sure sign of this in the gospels is the continuing companionship of Jesus with his friends — a company of love, a community of concern. The one clear sign of not rising from the dead is refusing to choose life; living now as if half dead, as if without hope.

> Gather gladness from the skies;
> Take a lesson from the ground;
> Flowers do ope their heavenward eyes
> And a Springtime joy have found;
> Earth throws her winter robes away,
> Decks herself for Easter Day.

Our lives as Christians are filled with ambiguity and uncertainty, but they at least have a starting point. It is that Jesus died and rose, and that he is Lord. On that cornerstone all else is built. There is an ethic, a theology, there are endless elaborations, but there is first a foundation. The just one, the innocent sufferer, the obedient servant *lives*. There is a little more to it than that. Nowhere in the gospels is Jesus' resurrection proclaimed as a private joy, a treasure of the hearer only. There is in every instance an obligation incurred, a charge attached. John tells of a Magdalene who gave the word she was entrusted with. "I have seen the Lord," she said. In Mark it goes tragically otherwise: "They made their way out and fled from the tomb bewildered and trembling; and they said nothing to anyone because they were afraid...."

That unfinished ending is the genius of Mark with its tale of a challenge unaccepted, even by Jesus' dearest familiars, out of fear. The message is clear. Spread the word, tell it, or the message dies. Yes, Jesus dies if no one believes it, no one lives it. For Easter is real only if it is taken seriously, only if Christ lives in us. Otherwise all is myth and fable. Cruel myth, ugly fable. But if he lives in any of us, the whole report is believable.

> Seek God's house in happy throng;
> Crowded let his table be;
> Mingle praises, prayer and song,
> Singing to the Trinity.
> Henceforth let your souls alway
> Make each morn an Easter day.

April 11, 1982   St. Paul's Parish

EASTER SUNDAY
Ac 10:34a, 37-43; 1 Cor 5:6b-8; Jn 20:1-9

Milano is a great modern city. Its handsome medieval cathedral rises improbably out of a sea of concrete and street railways. Only the piazza before it gives some sense of relief by its spaciousness. Beneath this open space, in the vicinity of the facade and church porch, there is a handsome excavation not yet twenty years old. Descent into it reveals the lineaments of

the baptistry and modest basilica from St. Ambrose's day
—the late fourth century. In the baptistry one sees, in very
good condition, the mosaic piscina or bath with its three
double steps like a stile. Into this pool Augustine stepped to be
baptized.

He was a young professor of rhetoric. His parents had
deferred his baptism, in the custom that lasted a century or so,
until the carnal sins of young manhood should be behind him.
Augustine had kept a mistress, sired a son, and drifted into a
heresy that seemed to him more intellectual than Catholicity.
Ultimately, Manicheism put a terrible strain on the credulity
of this young intellectual.

Augustine made a sort of retreat in a country place at the
end of the vintage vacation. His mother was along as well as
his soulmate, a certain Alypius. Augustine had asked Ambrose
what to read to prepare and had been told the book of Isaiah. It
is a comfort to us to learn he did not understand the earlier
part of it very well and so gave it up.

He turned in the three names for baptism — his own, his
son's, and his friend's — and waited meditating on the
mystery that a parent and a fifteen-year-old child could be the
same age in grace. "And we were baptized, and all anxiety as to
our past life fled away."

You might have expected from Augustine, if you knew the
delight he took in anguish and introspection, some deep
musings on the relation between sin and grace, burial in the
waters with Christ and future resurrection with him, slavery
and freedom. Instead he records the sacramental fact laconi-
cally, much as the evangelists record the death of Jesus.

What Augustine *does* record is the relation between salvation and song. Listen:

The days were not long enough as I meditated, and found wonderful delight in meditating, upon the depth of your design for the human race. I wept at the beauty of your hymns and canticles and was powerfully moved at the sweet sound of the church's singing. Those sounds flowed into my ears and the truth streamed into my heart; so that my feeling of devotion overflowed and the tears ran from my eyes, and I was happy in them.   (Augustine, *Confessions*)

Consider what this means. The man has a towering intellect. He has given up after years of struggle. A book of prophecy suggested to help him has proved too much for him. But he listens to the psalmody of praise and he cries.

There have been some tears in this church this evening. Some are new in Christ with the innocence of babes, others new in this Christian communion. We do not know all of their spiritual journey, but by their example we have been moved to contemplate our own. The Scriptures we venerate have been read out in solemn sequence —sometimes consoling, more often puzzling, as they were even for the learned Augustine. The mortar between the biblical cracks has been the song: plaintive psalms, joyous psalms, stately hymns, sprightly canticles. What we cannot express we sing. Despite our musical drawbacks as a congregation or as individuals we know that this language alone can convey what is in our hearts. We had been dead and we came to life. Only music can express it.

This same Augustine later wrote: "Whoever sings prays twice."

Luke tells a tale that is the story of our lives: believing women, resistant men. Peter, always the "takeover" type, checks for himself the story that seemed like nonsense to him.

Nothing like seeing for yourself. Try anything but relying on women. Such is the story of all the churches from Jesus' rising from the dead until now.

Paul attacks the problem another way. No narrative, with or without details, for him. Only the mind-arresting fact. Death, which leaves the victim quit of all obligations, achieves this in us: it puts us out of misery, out of slavery, out of the pain of life. How else describe the chains that bound us, the simple condition of human be-ing which Paul sums up as "sin"? There may have been wrongdoing aplenty, moral lapse on the grand scale, but Paul is not especially concerned about them. He has larger fish to fry. Even Augustine's self-centeredness as a mama's boy of thirty-three, his childish fixation with his passionate nature, are insignificant next to what Paul is talking about.

Paul is lost in wonder at the marvel of new beginning — the old creature and the new, the dead husk and the fresh grain, the corpse behind and the living Christ in us before.

So sing *Alleluia* whether you do it like Sills or Pavarotti or croak it like a crow. In or out of tune, it will make sweet music tonight. Let the sounds flow into our ears and the truth stream into our hearts. And do not be afraid to cry. If you are a new creature in Christ you will be happy in your tears.

April 10, 1983   St. Charles Borromeo Parish,
                             Montgomery Township, N.J.

THE FIFTY DAYS OF EASTER

SECOND SUNDAY OF EASTER
Ac 2:42-47; 1 Pt 1:3-9; Jn 20:19-31/Year A

Last Sunday — you may recall it — the heavens were opened. The weather here made Noah and Elijah who both experienced a little rain in their time look like desert nomads. It took some faith in the weatherman to believe that the sun would ever shine again. But by Monday, sure enough, and throughout the week the Eastern United States was sun-kissed handsomely. But I saw a newspaper editorial yesterday that said: "March had slush in its heart."

In today's gospel we are told something about Easter faith. This is a topic that goes far deeper in our lives than an everyday occurrence like the weather. The evangelist John wishes to convey to his contemporaries that seeing Jesus risen — actually experiencing him back from the dead — is a far lesser matter than believing in him as the risen one. It is as if I were to say to you: "Rejoicing in spring on a day like today is easy. It takes no imagination at all. But walking out into the downpour of last Sunday and saying to yourself: 'It's spring'! That took a little overcoming of the data of your senses."

The fourth gospel likes to take innocent bystanders and use them as foils to make its point. For John, Jesus is "the son" with respect to God. He gets all the best lines. Thomas — whose name we don't even know, since like "Didymus" in Greek it is just the word for a twin — Thomas ends up in John's gospel as the classic doubter. Was he really a skeptic, as hardheaded as he is made to sound? As a matter of history there is no way of knowing. The evangelist needs him for a different purpose. Thomas is not resisting the report of his friends on that first Easter night so much as representing us all over the ages. If he can set a condition for his belief he will not have to make any emotional investment in it. He can come off looking reasonable and detached. It is the relief we all crave from a heavy commitment. Cool, like Bogey, and getting Bacall in the bargain. "Unless I touch the wounds in his hands, unless I put my hand in his side . . . ." Conditions. You can put deciding off for a long time with conditions.

For the Christians of the apostolic age, believing that Jesus lived again was not a theoretical question. It was the living of a life. I do not mean that resurrection was an occurrence they took in stride. It was as unique then as it is now. Unique literally means "only once." You could not, however, get the early disciples interested in a discussion of amino acids and the irreversible process of decomposition. It was not because they were pre-scientific. It was because they went deeper than we. We can only ask: "Did it happen?" They went a step beyond: "If it happened what are its consequences? What must I do about it, supposing that it's true?"

Poor Thomas will take such a thumping today in the pulpits of the world that we ought to say a brief, kind word for doubt to right the balance. Where would any of us be, after all, if there were no doubters, none who withheld their judgment until all the evidence was in? Every one of us has suffered at the hands of people who get all their exercise jumping to conclusions. Doubt has a healthy quality about it if it looks for sufficient reasons and then acts once it thinks it has them.

What is a sufficient reason for believing in the resurrection? The gospel writer dismisses empirical evidence. Seeing is not believing, he says. It is the very opposite of believing. "Blessed are they who have not seen and have believed." We know from the rest of his gospel, not this passage only, that the word Jesus speaks is what puts this wonder beyond doubt. This truthful speaker is the one authenticating sign.

But, by definition, Jesus is not present to us to speak the truth. If he were we would only have to decide if his word sounded like God's truth to us. The first two readings put the matter squarely. Have you known the support of a community of believers that has made a risen Christ credible to you? The sharing of goods and property, meals taken in common, the breaking of bread and prayers? Experience that and you can believe in a dead man who walks the earth. Churches are empty because it was said once that Christian life meant support in time of need and it did not turn out to be that way: only silence, judgment, censure. Conversely, some very sophisticated persons are celebrating today their rebirth to salvation — not seated at home, in the midst of their textbooks of physics or economics or *The Washington Post* and *New York Times* all day — but gathered in the midst of warm friends who are praising God for his great mercy. The resurrection — Christ's in reality and ours in hope — is not a proposition to be judged and accepted. It is a life to be lived.

"Blessed are they who have not seen and have believed" — who have not seen the risen Christ, to be sure, but who have experienced him in the saints, the company of believers. Faith without experience of the love of others is a clear impossibility. With that experience it is possible to believe all things, even that Jesus Christ crucified lives.

April 2, 1978   St. Stephen Martyr Parish

SECOND SUNDAY OF EASTER
Ac 4:32-35; 1 Jn 5:1-6; Jn 20:19-31/Year B

The concluding phrases of today's gospel reading give every indication of once having been the final words of the fourth gospel with Chapter 21 added by the final editor. Jesus performed many signs, the original author maintains — many "other signs" besides his appearance to Thomas. They have been recorded to help us believe and believing have life in his name.

We call the sacraments "signs" although not exactly in the Johannine sense. A Christian life is a life of signs: baptism, many eucharists, marriage, the anointing of the sick perhaps more than once. They are properly speaking signs of faith, for without a personal trust-relation with God for his deed in Christ underlying them they are so much empty ritual. It is our reliance on God and on each other to sustain us that makes these signs effective. Rite of itself may merely root us in the familiar. It is only when it is based on a genuine sense of dependence that it can be thought of as a means of grace.

This faith of ours is an awareness of being begotten by God through love. The author of 1 John identifies faith as the power that has conquered the world. It is the conviction that we belong to a family of believers, that we are in the strict sense his "children." As long as we remain such we are immune from contempt or disregard for God.

There is such a thing as a thoughtless faith. There is even an arrogant faith — an unconscious scorn for others not as blessed as we. Needless to say it does not befit a Christian. "Faith that does not perpetually expose itself to the possibility of unfaith," a philosopher has written, "is no faith but merely a convenience" (Martin Heidegger, *Introduction to Metaphysics,* p. 7). A believer in sacraments runs the risk of spiritual sloth. Ours is an institutional worship and if we partake in it regularly we may be guilty of the smugness of self-comfort. We can be nourished before we experience hunger and thirst, thus dulling our taste. Meanwhile other searchers, other seekers, make the most of the signs they have. These prove to be richer vehicles of grace for them than the eucharistic body of the Lord for us. God's "real absence" can in some circumstances prove a better spur than the Son's "real presence." Trust in whoever God may be, wherever he means to lead, empowers some to articulate their search for truth. "If you had not found me you could never seek me," Augustine wrote long ago addressing himself to God. Faith is a strange world of quest where the seekers have arrived and those who search not, question not, doubt not have no place to go.

Jesus came in water and in blood. It is the Spirit who testifies to this. The reality of Jesus in the flesh began with his baptism and ended with his death on the cross. Unless one believes in the historical truth of what lay between these two events one lacks faith in God's essential deed. He was sent by the Father and in turn sent the Spirit, the breath of God, to achieve our forgiveness. Membership in the community of faith means belonging to a family in which our sins can be taken away. We are forgiven and forgive one another. We have a place to lay down our burden of guilt.

All these matters have a special meaning to us in this season of signs of our faith. Last Sunday we renewed our baptismal commitment because Easter was the ancient day of adult entry into the church. This week was the first week of life for many around the globe who are "new in Christ." Either they were baptized or they renewed a commitment made for them in infancy by professing Catholic faith. Next came the comple- tion of that rite, the sealing of the Spirit or "chrismation." A bishop was not required to administer it. The priest who baptized them or received their profession of faith was capable. Finally, they ate and drank the Lord's body in the ancient eucharistic rite at Easter Mass.

I am describing the conclusion of the restored rite of Christian initiation which begins with enrollment in the catechumenate and ends — two years or more later — on the great night of Easter. Most of us were confirmed some time between the ages of eight and twelve in a rite that got separated in the West from the baptism of which it was integrally a part. It became the occasion for the bishop's visitation and later took on an ambivalent character. Confirmation became a rite of Christian maturity, a strengthening of faith against resist- ance and attack, a more intense gift of the Spirit. But all of these significations were contrived once the imposing of hands and chrismation had lost their moorings in the initiation rite as the completion of baptism before one's first reception of the Eucharist.

Confirmation is emerging as a rite of commitment in high adolescence or young adulthood in some quarters. This is a laudable development as to intent, I suppose. But anything that separates it from its historical place as a sealing of the Spirit preparatory to a lifetime of eucharistic reception cannot be totally praiseworthy. The Rite of Christian Initiation for Adults will surely prevail in time for adolescents, children and babies. I am speaking of all three signs of beginning a life in Christ being kept together whenever administered. This could mean a reception of confirmation and eucharist together in early childhood (a custom we had in this country earlier in this century). Something like a lenten catechesis could serve as an invitation to the commitments to Christ proper to subsequent ages of development. No sacrament other than the Eucharist is needed for such a rite of passage. Or there could be in time the enrollment of catechumens in infancy, since birth into a believing, practicing family makes one a Christian, with the three sacraments of initiation marked by an appropriate catechesis administered at some later time. Ever since A.D. 175 we have been baptizing infants but this practice presumably preceded it.

What matters is that we know that our initiatory rites are signs of our Easter faith. They are public, not private. They touch the life of the whole church community. Anything we do about these rites that brings this home to us makes us that much more Christian.

April 22, 1979   St. Stephen Martyr Parish

SECOND SUNDAY OF EASTER
Ac 5:12-16; Rev 1:9-13, 17-19; Jn 20:19-31/Year C

There were years in Ireland in the past, as in many places under repressive dictatorship now, when Catholic faith had to go underground. The faithful gathered on the mountainsides or in the glens and in the forests in secret at Mass rocks, some of which are still visited today. Nature itself became the hidden cathedral and secret churches. Of that day — and it is not so many centuries past — a modern poet Patrick Kavanagh has written of his fellow farmers:

Yet sometimes when the sun comes through a gap
these men know God the Father in a tree:
the Holy Spirit in the rising sap,
And Christ will be
in the green leaves that will come at Easter
from the sealed and guarded tomb.

The sealed and guarded tomb of course was Ireland — all
political poetry is cryptic — and Easter with Christ coming
forth in the green leaves was the day of future deliverance. Has
that day come? If you know the history of that troubled island
I ask you to judge for yourself. This much at least can be said:
the history of violence among Christians around the globe is
such that the continuing power of sin is absolutely clear. Jesus
has come forth from the tomb as a reality of the first century
yet is still imprisoned there by all who proclaim his resurrection religiously while denying it humanly.

I speak as somberly as I do on the eighth day of the feast
—the Second Sunday of Easter, as it is newly named among
us — because the church that we are lives forever with a
painful paradox. On the Lord's day we "proclaim God's word
and bear witness to Jesus" (Rev 1:9). "One like a son of man"
touches us at this liturgy and tells us: "There is nothing to fear.
I am the first and last, the living one. Once I was dead but now
I live, forever and ever. I hold the keys of death and the nether
world." Yet we are conscious that if he is not alive in us his
livingness at God's right hand is of no consequence. He
conquers death and hell only if we let him do so in us. If we
perpetuate wars and killings, starve the poor, damage reputa-
tions, warp the young, then we engage in the rhetoric of
religion without doing the works of religion. We proclaim
faith while perverting faith, sing "Hosanna" and "Alleluia"
while bringing down on ourselves a curse and not a blessing.

Surely such is the intent of no one here. Yet we must remind ourselves of the perilousness of our Easter profession, the awesomeness of our hope that "men and women in great numbers [will be] continually added to the Lord" (Ac 5:14). It must be a good for the world that there are Christians. Is it? Are there among us the signs of the apostles — healings, cures, the soothing of troubled spirits? Does Easter mean the walking abroad on the earth of the risen Lord in us in whom he lives?

The fact must be faced, I think, that faith progressively loses its grip on the world's population as the world becomes increasingly secularized. By that I mean that less and less does religion provide answers to the questions people are asking. They have increasingly less need of it as they see the responses to their needs met in other ways: by the food they require, the technical progress that gives them a better life, the recreations and the sports and the arts however debased that provide relief from daily drudgery. Religious people like to suppose that the great mystery of life and death is met by none of these things, that eternal hungers continue so long as mortality persists. It may very well not be so. If it were, the Christian churches of the globe would be filled every Sunday because they proclaim hope in what is humanity's greatest problem. But they are not filled. The fact of having to die is probably not humanity's greatest problem.

Having to live is. We see the mosques and public squares of the Muslim world, the rivers and temples of the Hindu world, the wayside shrines and monasteries of the Buddhist world filled with the devout because the multitudes gain there some help for living. As the standard of living rises and village clinics multiply and the Sonys and Fiats cover the earth the petitions and the prayers slacken off and the pieties become a memory — a cherished memory, perhaps, but a memory.

Can Christian faith resist such cultural erosions? It seems no better able to than the other faiths, despite all our claims for the greatness of Jesus. We call him Lord and Christ, the bridge between heaven and earth, God with us. Yet the churches empty out, indifference to religion multiplies, an unfriendly Islam both Shi'ite and Sunni accuses us Christians of having forfeited all faith in God in our pursuit of gain. The root question is, I think, has the risen Lord anything to say about the living of a life? For, in fact, his triumph over death seems to be a matter in which the Christian world has a very modest interest.

"Jesus came and stood before them. 'Peace be with you,' he said" (Jn 20:19). Then he sent his disciples out with a task, even as God had sent him. He breathed upon them the breath of God making them the agents of divine forgiveness — or its withholding if there is no change of heart. "Do not persist in your unbelief but believe. . . . Blest are they who have not seen and have believed" (vv. 27c, 29b).

The resurrection of Jesus, therefore, is all about a lived human life. It is about nothing else. It holds out the possibility of peace where there is no peace, of mutual forgiveness in a community that is defined as a forgiving community. Is there a proved human need for these tremendous gifts? I think you can say that a war-torn and starving and exploited and anxious and unreconciled human family needs nothing so sorely as what the risen Christ stands ready to give — if we who have not seen will only believe.

April 13, 1980   St. Stephen Martyr Parish

THIRD SUNDAY OF EASTER
Ac 2:14, 22-28; 1 Pt 1:17-21; Lk 24:13-35/Year A

If we wish to know how Christ's resurrection was preached in the earliest church we have to turn to St. Paul's report of the tradition in 1 Corinthians 15 starting at the beginning of the chapter. He is writing in the year 55 or so, hence twenty-five years after Jesus' death. The previous two chapters have been on the greatest of gifts, charity, and immediately in its wake "prophecy," by which Paul means clear teaching. He then goes to the heart of "the gospel which I preached to you" because the Corinthians seem to be all enthused by peripheral matters: speaking in tongues, the "wisdom" of high-flown discourse, a "spiritual" existence and the like. What is "the gospel" that he first received, then handed on unaltered?

—That Christ died for our sins, in accordance with the Scriptures;

—that he was buried and, according to the Scriptures, rose on the third day;

—that he was seen by Cephas [Rock], then by the Twelve;

—after that he was seen by 500 believers at once, of whom most are still alive but some have fallen asleep;

—next he was seen by James, then by all the apostles (3b-7).

Paul then departs from the familiar script and slips into what he is equally interested in reminding the Corinthians of —that the risen Christ was, last of all, seen by him some three or four years later. Whether people hear the gospel from Paul or other accredited apostolic witnesses, "this is what we preached and this is what you believed" (v. 11). It is important to recall at this season that to be a Christian is not just to believe in God but in the God who raised up the son Jesus Christ from the dead.

Well, if the earliest proclamation of the resurrection that we have any record of was an unelaborated account of death, burial, and rising; if the witnesses were Peter, the Twelve, a great number, then James and all the apostles, how account for the marvelous tales we are so familiar with? They have a different cast of characters altogether. The holy women racing to the tomb. An angel breaking the news — or was it two? Or was it a young man — or two young men? The story of Thomas the doubter and the Magdalene who mistook Jesus for the gardener and Cleopas and his companion in today's narrative? Where did all these tales come from?

St. Paul in all his correspondence never reports on Jesus' resurrection as an event with a value or importance of its own. It always has significance as the cause of a greater marvel —the new life in Christ of the believer. The resurrection is at the heart of his gospel — and he does not provide a scrap of information about it.

Well, you say, narrative was not his form. He composed no gospel like the four the church retained. That must be the difference. Still, Paul was not so poor in word power or detail that he could not have done a superb piece of work in describing those first days and hours of new, risen life.

The reasons for Paul's silence are probably two: the narratives we read on these Sundays had not been developed yet when he wrote; and even if he heard fragments of them on the two occasions he visited Jerusalem he might have thought them too detailed — too interested in who saw what, when, and how. Paul believed that there were certain witnesses more favored than others; "apostles," he called them and he was one of them. Yet those who had not seen and believed were his major interest: the pagan Godfearers of far off Asia Minor, Greece and Italy whose faith could not depend on being close to the historical events. Paul was concerned, in brief, for all of us. Our faith does not stand or fall on grasping Jesus firmly in embrace and being told to let go. It has nothing to do with a clear memory of all the events in Jerusalem over the past few days. We believe because a whole chain of witnesses attests to the fact going back to Peter, James, and Paul. "The Lord has been raised. It is true. He has appeared to Simon" (Lk 22:34). We know him in the breaking of bread.

We make Eucharist together and the risen Lord is in our midst. We do deeds of self-effacing service and the report of his new life becomes credible. We crush in ourselves the love of death — the war machine, on which the people's voice has been terrifyingly silent these hundred days since Inauguration Day; the craven deemphasis on the rights of oppressed peoples in the interests of our economy, our markets; the abortion industry, which our whole life as a nation has made an attractive alternative — all this love of death we must put to death or Christ will never live in us. What does his brief life of forty days mean as demonstration, proof, or show if it is not blazoned forth in lives of faith? It means that he lives in our lives or it means nothing.

Here is the way St. John Chrysostom put the reality of the Easter season decades ago:

> Whoever you are, come,
>   celebrate this shining happening,
>   this festival of light.
> You the devout, God's unshakable lover,
>   and you the servant brimming with thanks.
> Come, walk into the joy of your Lord.
> And you the impoverished faster, come for your wages.
> You who began before sunrise, come for your stipend.

You who waited till nine in the morning: the feast is for *you.*
And you, the not-till-noonday starter,
   do not hesitate; you shall not lose a thing.
You who began at only three in the afternoon,
   have no scruples, come.
And you who arrived just before sunset,
   forget you were late. Do not be bashful.
Our Master is magnanimous and welcomes
   the very latest with the very first.
He will not entertain you less, you of the eleventh hour,
   than you the dawn toiler. No, not at all.
To this one he gives, and on that one he showers rewards.
Whether you were a success or whether you only tried,
   he will greet you, make much of your effort,
      extol your intention.

Let everybody, therefore, crowd into the exhilaration of our
   Savior.
You the first and you the last: equally heaped with blessings.
You the rich and you the poor: celebrate together.
You the careful and you the careless: enjoy this day of days.
You that have kept the fast, and you that have broken it:
   be happy today.
The table is loaded. Feast on it like princes.
The milkfed veal is fat. Let no one go hungry.
And drink, all of you: drink the cup. The vintage is faith.
Feed sumptuously all: feed on his goodness, his sheer
   abundance.
No one need think he is poor,
   for the universal empire is emblazoned, wide open for all.
No one need mourn uncountable falls, be they over and
   over.

For forgiveness itself has reared from the tomb.

No one need fear death; for our Savior himself has died
and set us free.

He confronted death in his own person, and blasted it to
nothing.

He made it defunct by the very taste of his flesh.

This is exactly what Isaiah foretold when he declared:

"Hell is harrowed by encounter with *him.*"

Of course it is harrowed.

For now hell is a joke, finished, done with.

Harrowed because now taken prisoner.

It snatched at a body and — incredible — lit upon God.

It gulped down the earth, and gagged on heaven.

It seized what it saw, and was crushed by what it failed to see.

Poor death, where is your sting?

Poor hell, where is your triumph?

Christ steps out of the tomb and you are reduced to nothing.

Christ rises and the angels are wild with delight.

Christ rises and the graves are emptied of dead.

Oh yes, for he broke from the tomb like a flower,
a beautiful fruit:

the first fruit of those already gone.

All glory be his, all success and power. . .for ever and ever.

(New translation by Paul Roche)

May 3, 1981   St. Paul's Parish

THIRD SUNDAY OF EASTER
Ac 3:13-15, 17-19; 1 Jn 2:1-5; Lk 24:35-48/Year B

I am teaching a course this semester at Temple University in the doctrinal structure of Christianity. The students include four young American Jews (three of them candidates for the rabbinate), a woman from North India who is a Sikh, a Buddhist monk from Sri Lanka, and five men from Muslim countries who are already on university faculties. There are also a few Christians enrolled who have never had a college-level course in the faith they profess. All read the entire New Testament in mid-January and have been consulting it ever since in conjunction with second- to twentieth-century readings.

It is a pleasure to lead this seminar because of the high interest of all the members in what Christianity teaches. The challenge is different from that of being your preacher at St. Paul's where we profess a common Catholic faith. Here I am charged with stirring up the faith you have held from childhood and in the process renewing my own. But the students are in a quite different condition. They find it easy to admire Jesus in everything he teaches. All the non-Christians in the group have heard that we adore Jesus Christ as the son of God and very God. They are surprised that the New Testament does not say this on every page; that he is God on any page. The Jews and Muslims come thinking we have a soft policy on the undivided unity of God. They are convinced that we have introduced plurality into deity and are suspicious of the landmark Christian creeds that say it is not so. The subtlety of our belief in a triune God, about which not even we presume to have comprehensive knowledge, absorbs much of their intellectual energies.

But the great question is the one which we have proposed to us in today's three readings in the Easter season. What do we mean when we say that we believe the whole world is redeemed — or can be — by faith in Jesus Christ crucified and risen? The question is of utmost importance to us Christians. It is likewise a delicate matter to convey to non-Christians, all of whom have long suffered under a Christian colonialism and proselytism exercised by Christians more concerned with gold than God, with political oppression than religious faith. How would you explain to a non-Christian neighbor what you are convinced God did for all humanity in Jesus Christ?

We know the way Luke expressed it in the book of Acts and 1 John (whoever wrote that epistle) and Luke in his gospel. For the earliest preachers whose teaching the New Testament records, Jesus is the servant of the LORD, the one who led the way to life, a prophet God raised from the dead. He is the just intercessor for us with God, the offering for the sins of the whole world. Jesus is the fulfillment of all promise in Scripture. He is the one who had to suffer and rise, the person in whose name remission of sins must be preached.

How does one speak of these things to a Buddhist who believes in the harmony of the universe but not in a creator God, to a Muslim or a Jew convinced that any intermediary with God threatens the awe-full sovereignty of the One who alone is God? How indeed does one speak of these things in the midst of a Christian assembly like this one?

In our seminar we have let many voices speak over the last four months. Saints Ignatius of Antioch and Augustine, Anselm and Aquinas, Martin Luther and John Calvin. Just on Thursday past all had read a book by a German priest named

Rahner called *Our Christian Faith*. On the central Christian matter of Jesus as savior he writes:

> What we have here is not just a human being who, through a death accepted without reserve, himself discovered God's freedom. That much we may hope [for] from the death of every human being in the long history of the human race. But that the death of some other person means for me a promise from God himself — that, we can know in faith of no other death than that of Jesus. For, in the case of other people, how can we know that they are dying in solidarity with me, that they...wish to obtain their salvation from [knowing] God in all his incomprehensibility only if, and insofar as, this wish means me too and not just them? Of what other human being except Jesus can we know, in faith, that the surrender of death was an act of unconditional trust and not an ultimate despair at the disappearance of all [human] support? Where except in Jesus' resurrection, can I find the certainty that this surrender of his means nothing other than the victorious outcome of his death ....His victorious death is fulfillment and...this fulfillment makes God's saving will...irreversible. The death of Jesus is the manifestation in human history of this fulfillment, hence the effect of grace and the cause of grace whereby God is always and everywhere the deepest energy and force in his salvation [call it redemption, call it liberation — of the world he created in love].

Can I put it more simply? The cross is the world's sole great human surrender in death, in utter trust for us. The resurrection is God's testimony that the offer on our behalf has been received. His gracious love for us went uninterrupted by cross and resurrection but never has it been so clearly manifest before or since.

We need to make an Easter prayer of thanksgiving for all that has been done for us. Let us join Blessed Juliana of Norwich, who manages somehow to put things just right:

It is [Christ Jesus'] office to save us. It is his glory to do it. And it is His will that we know this. For He willeth that we love Him sweetly and trust in Him meekly and mightily.

There was nothing else I could tell my students. I did not try to win their favor, nor could I assure them that Christianity makes no special claims. There was no way around it. To be Christian is to believe that the God who is Lover of all has done something unique in human history to prove he is Lover of all.

April 25, 1982   St. Paul's Parish

THIRD SUNDAY OF EASTER
Ac 5:27b-32, 40b-41; Rev 5:11-14; Jn 21:1-19/Year C

The New Testament has always been interpreted to suit people's political, theological, and economic views. But it does not exist to accommodate our prejudices, it exists to pass judgment on us. Jesus is not someone we are free to remake in our own image and liking. We must try to find out who he is and to conform ourselves to him, not him to us.

Since 1900 there have been efforts to make Jesus a revolutionist and to interpret his sayings as in agreement with the Zealots of his time, the radical group that demanded war with Rome and independence for the Jews. In this modern revolutionary period, many have claimed Jesus as one of their historical leaders, a champion of freedom against repressive governments. But the tradition found in the gospels does not sustain this thesis. Jesus emerges as quite independent of revolution. Nonetheless, he did fall afoul of powerful forces which destroyed him. Why? It would appear that they could not endure the stands he took in conscience.

He was "the Lamb that was slain," for the author of the book of Revelation, the "One seated on the throne" to whom are "praise and honor, glory and might." But all those accolades came later. On the afternoon he was killed he was just one more innocent Jew going to his death for being true to himself and to his purpose. He had not preached revolt or violence. His call was for a new life in preparation for the coming judgment and the New Age. We must describe him as religiously oriented. Political he was not. Yet he was political because he cared for the honor of his Father and the rights of his fellow creatures. Peter and the apostles gave testimony to the risen Christ only because he had testified to the truth before them. The charge against them in their turn was that in their preaching they were making the authorities responsible for his blood. They did no such thing. They simply continued to fill Jerusalem with his teaching — religious teaching — and no other conclusion could be drawn but that they spread his mischief. The authorities had silenced him; therefore all these efforts to silence Peter and the others.

Our attorney general did a frightening thing on Friday night. He hinted at violence in Washington for yesterday's demonstration — but 300,000 people left the tulips on the Capitol lawn undisturbed. The government piously says that its sole concern in the peace movement is with the spread of violence. But bringing an end to war is a violation of the will to continue it. Therefore every successful attempt to educate people about the horror of war must be put in a bad light. Otherwise, they and their sons might refuse to fight.

Just as Jesus' followers after his resurrection were peaceful people, though they had it in common with revolutionaries that they embarrassed governments, so Jesus' followers committed to peace today abhor violence but must be made to look violent because they embarrass governments.

Anyone who has seen a thing at first hand speaks with authority about it. The soldier speaks convincingly of the terror of battle provided all boasting is absent. Alcoholism is described most accurately by members of Alcoholics Anonymous. It is not enough to be or to have been a heavy drinker; there must be joined to this a passion for truth about one's drinking.

Today's gospel is written with the authority of witnesses to the resurrection. The author knew how difficult it would be for hearers to believe his story. Therefore he tells how the disciples themselves did not believe it until they saw him. They had breakfast with him, witnessed the power of his earthly life renewed, and recognized him in the familiar way he broke bread with them. "Do you love me?. . .Feed my lambs." They became so convinced that Jesus was living that they were willing, even glad, to risk their lives to proclaim that good news.

We sit here today as believers, as recipients of the heritage of the gospel because someone had the courage to give witness to it for us. Whether we are black or white we enjoy such liberty as we have because someone committed to justice fought and died for it. If this war we are in ever ends it will be as a result not of government efforts or announced dates of troop pullouts but of the voices for peace that would not be stilled.

Up until now it has been relatively easy for the government to call the protestors peaceniks and longhairs and kooks. It gets harder and harder to do that. Yesterday's demonstration had a much more mature character — I speak of the age of the crowd, not its opinions. For the first time there were sizable numbers of black people. And above all there was the impact of the veterans giving their testimony. Limbs missing, wheelchairs rolling, medals flung onto the Capitol lawn. Frustrated, angry, generous citizens trying to say to deaf ears, "Feed the sheep."

April 25, 1971   Our Lady of Mercy Parish

FOURTH SUNDAY OF EASTER
Ac 4:8-12; 1 Jn 3:1-2; Jn 10:11-18/Year B

Senator William Proxmire of Wisconsin has accomplished much on the national scene but he is probably best known for his monthly Golden Fleece award. He gets staff members to sniff out the expenditure of taxpayers' money for foolish, needless or wasteful purposes. Sometimes the award backfires. Invariably the recipient cries "Foul!" But the American taxpayer, John Q. Public naked in his barrel, is so used to being fleeced that he forgives the Senator's rate of probable error and thanks him for the service.

The source in the Bible for all New Testament references to sheep and shepherds is Ezekiel 34:

> Son of man [the word of the Lord came to the prophet], prophesy against the shepherds of Israel. . . . Woe to [them] who have been pasturing themselves. Should not shepherds, rather, pasture sheep? You have fed off their milk, worn their wool, and slaughtered the fatlings, but the sheep you have not pastured. You did not strengthen the weak nor heal the sick nor bind up the injured. . . . You lorded it over them harshly and brutally. So they were scattered for lack of a shepherd, and became food for all the wild beasts (vv. 2-5).

And so the diatribe goes on, leading to the promise of one shepherd over them to pasture them and be their guide. He is "my servant David, who shall be prince among them" (vv. 23, 24). Well, David had been dead for 400 years when Ezekiel wrote, so a promise regarding the future must have been intended.

That is why the evangelist John felt so secure in portraying Jesus as the virtuous or good shepherd. Believing in him as risen from the dead, he knew the use God had put him to in the service of the many. John changes Ezekiel's harsh assessment of Israel's political leaders — its weak and avaricious kings — to a description of religious leaders. Exactly who they were we do not know. They are "hirelings," hence leaders of

Christian groups because contrasted with the "thieves and marauders" of earlier in the chapter, non-community members who prey on the sheepfold by coming in from outside. Perhaps the hirelings are those who "believed in Jesus" (8:31) but wrongly by the evangelist's standard, against whom much of his gospel is directed.

We know from second-century writings about groups of Christian Jews who reverenced Jesus as a teacher but would not allow the claim that his person was a full expression of godhead — the very claim made by John's gospel. They adopted the sacred meal of Christians but thought of it in terms of fellowship, not of a sacrament of the body and blood of the Lord as St. Ignatius of Antioch did. So, already in New Testament times it seems, believers in Jesus are divided over who he is and what he does. There are "my sheep" — the John believers — and "other sheep not of this fold." What are the differences between them? In the context of today's reading, the main one seems to be that Jesus lays his life down freely and takes it up again. He is not the victim of a Roman capital sentence but one who dies voluntarily in response to a command or charge of the Father. This freedom in "laying down" and "taking his life up again" divides Jesus' hearers in the way the Johannine discourses generally do. The evangelist says he writes his gospel so that people will take a stand on Jesus — belief or acceptance, light or darkness, life or condemnation.

Familiarity with two generations of hirelings in church and state can tarnish the image of shepherds and sheep. I have been immensely heartened by the faithful silent men I have seen in Turkey, Greece, Israel and Algeria who are out there with their flocks in the heat of day or the black of night whether there is anyone to see them or not. The image is powerful. They are faithful. The lives of the sheep are *their* life.

The Easter mystery is still uppermost in our thoughts after three weeks. "There is no salvation in anyone else, for there is no other name in the whole world given to us by which we are to be saved" (Ac 4:12). "We are God's children now. What we shall be later has not yet come to light" (Jn 3:2). In Jesus Christ risen we live; we are guided, protected by the strong lover who cared enough for us to give his life. There have been many good shepherds since Jesus' day — selfless leaders, honest politicians, dedicated clergy — who have thought more of their people than of themselves. They are not a numerous crowd but they exist. Some heroic patriots and pastors have given their lives. So let us not say that Jesus' devotion has never been repeated in the world's history. It has.

The unique element is this. It was a death totally without regard to self — done only for the sake of others; and it was accepted by God, as the resurrection attests, in a way we know of in no other human self-giving.

We have a strong Shepherd who lives. Someone may be out to fleece us but it is not he.

Are we called to be sheep — poor defenseless beasts? Surely not that but defenders of the poor, givers of life. Like Jesus the Shepherd.

May 3, 1982   St. James Church

FOURTH SUNDAY OF EASTER

Ac 13:14, 43-52; Rev 7:9, 14-17; Jn 10:27-30/Year C

All the prayers and readings of today's liturgy come together in the theme of the good shepherd. Each liturgical season — Advent, Lent, Easter's Fifty Days, the time after Pentecost — returns again and again to Jesus under this image. The wise and gentle pedagogy of the liturgy always brings popular piety back to the good shepherd. The image, which John attributes to Jesus himself, affirms that *he* is the shepherd of Isaiah and Ezekiel, the upright, non-predatory ruler through whom God cares for the chosen people. It is a figure of concern for the defenseless, leadership to safety, the very opposite of taking advantage. Shepherds ultimately work for owners who derive their livelihoods from these dumb beasts — wool, lamb and mutton, parchment, lanolin. We all know that. It is no use to romanticize the grazing industry. But while the animals are in the shepherd's care they are assured life, growth, and security.

The opening prayer or collect of this morning integrated the readings and the entire Mass formulary. We are in a "valley of darkness eaten up by anxieties (that betray our lack of faith) and by resentments (that betray our lack of love)." Our first task, in the penitential rite, was to acknowledge the darkness and lostness to which we cling. The collect boldly affirms, "No evil shall we fear," because a shepherd has been sent for "our hope and strength." But unless we first bring our despair and weakness to the surface, the prayer is a meaningless formula. Forces beyond us are our daily experience. Global wars that are none of our making, whole corporations going under with job loss for laborers all the way up to executives, protracted strikes that eat up home ownership and all savings, drugs in the schools when we thought our children were immune. We can become comfortable in our desolation or at least at home with it. The Bible and the liturgy try to confront us with God's dream for us: to clothe us with hope, strength, joy; to wipe every tear from our eyes; to lead us to a state free from all anxiety. This is not a promise of an earthly paradise. Whoever thinks so misconstrues the Bible's message. But there is in Jesus Christ the promise of peace.

The first reading is a thoroughly idealized account of the new faith of pagan Greeks. It takes place in the city of Antioch in the province of Pisidia — the south-central Turkish highlands. They were delighted when they heard the Bible of the Jews quoted in their favor — Israel as a "light to the nations, a means of salvation to the ends of the earth." They responded to the word of the Lord with praise. Can you imagine their sense of lostness, despair and lovelessness turned to trust in the Good Shepherd who goes out precisely for what is lost?

The second reading affirms the consolation found in this valley of darkness. "The Lamb on the throne will shepherd them. He will lead them to springs of life-giving water, and God will wipe every tear from their eyes." The book of Revelation is easy to dismiss as an airy-fairy collection of visions. In an important sense it is the most hard-headed book in the New Testament. It faces the fact of Rome's hideous military and commercial power as none of the gospels or Paul or the men of his school do. Revelation's author knows that little people die for no good reason other than that power needs to consume them. The huge crowd in long white robes, palm branches in hand, are the "desaparecidos" whom the women and children of the Plaza de Mayo of Buenos Aires will not let the government forget, the Argentinians by the thousands who have sunk without a trace. The Caesars ate up human lives as the dictatorships of Central America do and the Soviets in Afghanistan and until recently Idi Amin in Uganda. The Christian prophet John of Patmos reminded a numbed, uncomprehending race of new believers: there is a Power stronger than power which has brought to its throne the innocent just, the victims of the Roman imperial war machine.

I have read the third draft of our bishops' message on war and peace lately, the one they shall be debating and voting on in Chicago May 2nd and 3rd. The eyes of people committed to peace the world over are trained on it, you may be sure, from Weinberger and Shultz to Andropov and John Paul. It has its shortcomings, as you may have read in *Time* or *The Monitor*, but you may be proud of it. Two themes emerge with total clarity: the fact of human sin with its resultant greed and lust for power has made of war a tragic necessity in every age; but in our time wars of obscene magnitude threaten to overtake us because we have trusted in the human capacity to avert them rather than pursuing peace through a God of peace. You may have derived the impression from the press that the document is an essay on strategies, political and military. It is not that. It is a powerful morality, an invitation to us the Catholic body U.S.A. to take the arts of peace seriously. It is a challenge to our nation which seems to be lacking in the will to peace through its elected officials.

The Pulitzer prizes in journalism were awarded last week. One went to an article in *Foreign Affairs* (60, 1982), entitled "Nuclear Weapons and the Atlantic Alliance" written by McGeorge Bundy, George Kennan our Princeton neighbor, Robert McNamara, and Gerard Smith. Smith is a Catholic but that is a detail of no consequence. This sentence from their article appears as footnote 61 [formerly 55]:

It is time to recognize that no one has ever succeeded in advancing any persuasive reason to believe that any use of nuclear weapons, even on the smallest scale, could reliably be expected to remain limited (p. 757).

The same note also contains a quote from General A.S. Collins, former deputy commander in chief of the U.S. Army in Europe:

From my experience in combat there is no way that [nuclear escalation]. . .can be controlled because of lack of information, the pressure of time and the deadly results that are taking place on both sides of the battle line (from J. F. Reichart and S. R. Sturn, eds., *American Defense Policy*, Baltimore, 1982.)

And from Harold Brown in his 1979 *Annual Report* as Secretary of Defense:

The odds are high, whether weapons were used against tactical or strategic targets, that control would be lost on both sides and the exchange would become unconstrained (Washington, U.S. Government Printing Office, 1979).

But they are footnotes. The body of the text is about religious faith — trust in God rather than armies, recourse to the Good Shepherd, the Lamb who was slain and who teaches the bold will to love that is the essence of God. We may not resist the image of God as the rescuer of humanity in its lostness, the shepherd who takes risks for his people and is wounded by briars in the search for what is lost. But we are not dumb sheep. We are thinking, willing people, whose will for peace may be no less than that of our God and his Christ.

April 24, 1983   St. James Church

FIFTH SUNDAY OF EASTER
Ac 6:1-7; 1 Pt 2:4-9; Jn 14:1-12/Year A

It was a sobering week. We almost lost the Pope although now it seems he will be spared to us.

No one in the Turkish government seems to be sure of the goals of the anti-Communist right-wing group to which the would-be assassin is said to belong. That troubled country has known little peace in the last two years. In six weeks in Germany last summer I learned that the Turkish politics of violence were being fought out daily in the Turkish press of West Germany, even though things are largely under control in the homeland. There are 1.3 million Muslim Turks in West Germany alone, not to speak of the numbers in Italy and France.

The pastor of Francis Hughes — the second hunger striker to die — said at his funeral in their small town thirty miles from Belfast that the Lord seemed very far from them these twelve years past. That took courage, I should think, with the Provos present in full uniform giving the appearance of a military funeral, rifles fired into the air at the agreed-upon distance from church and cemetery. And the grieving family sitting there, none too anxious to hear about a whole province's infidelity to the gospel.

The Syria-Israel War — there is no other name for it —grows hotter over the skies of victim Lebanon.

Here at home many people in their sixties and over got a jolt from a Social Security plan that is still in the White House handout-to-the-press stage. That was the good news. The bad news is that if it becomes law, and if the projected curbing of inflation does not go exactly according to schedule, the reduction for some will not be the ten percent proposed but will climb to twelve or fifteen.

Last Saturday I gave a talk at a brunch in the hotel where I had been a busboy in the summer of 1937 and was first issued a Social Security card. I got $12 a week before deductions. The group at lunch in the Molly Pitcher? Twenty resigned priests and their wives. There are about 11,000 in this country, not all married; the world figure is proportionate. I was thinking none of those thoughts when I worked there after my first year of college. Some of you have seen more than I have in the line of social change. What must it have been like to live through the Black Death, the Napoleonic years, Russia from the Czar through the revolution to the literal decimation of males in World War II — one dead in ten?

You may say philosophically that God has seen a lot in his time but the providential gaze can endure it. With poor weak humans who last seventy, eighty, ninety years it is another matter.

Is it another matter? Christians say no. We say that if you think that God knows nothing of our pain you have not begun to understand the incarnation. We do not hesitate to call the life of Jesus "the human history of God." He lived a short life of perfect trust in God and ended a victim of violence in one of history's many crossfires. St. Luke said in exculpation of Jesus' executioners, "They know not what they do" (23:34), but Jesus knew exactly what he was doing. He was drinking the cup of being fully human and trying to serve God in obedience.

Large parts of the Scriptures that we read out solemnly each Sunday in both testaments are a survival literature. Apart from Paul's seven universally acknowledged authentic letters, all of the New Testament was written after Jerusalem was destroyed and the temple flattened. Believers in Jesus were being harassed by Jews and Romans alike for two sets of reasons. Proclaim a crucified Messiah and see how popular you will be in Judaism. Tell the Roman empire that it has finished off your great one by the route of judicial murder and learn your survival chances as a "lawful religion," the status like Judaism's that you wish for.

Listen, then, with great care to these Easter season readings. They were all written to help people cope, literally to tough it out, survive.

Acts 6 tells the story of the first split in the early church. The Jerusalem community was divided along language lines, Hebrew- and Greek-speaking Jews, like the differences between Israelis of European and Moroccan or Yemenite origin. But the schism went much deeper than language. It was between the Seven and the Twelve — the Twelve standing for Jesus' intimates in life, Galilean to the core; the Seven the Stephen party, all Jews with Greek names but the last-named, Nicolaus, who is described as a pagan convert to Judaism. Can there, then, be trouble in paradise with the Lord not long risen from the tomb? Indeed there was. For the early church was not only born in pain of its mother, Judaism. It was born to twin Jewish cultures, the Hebrew and the Hellenist. The younger lived; it was the Greek-speaking church to which we belong. The older died, the Aramaic church of the Jameses and Andrew and Bartholomew of which we know almost nothing. All birth is pain. All growth is a daily dying.

The short snatch of 1 Peter is instructive. It tells Christians that humanity has little use for them. They are rejected, not only as Israel was in the psalmist's day, but now by Jew and gentile alike. With the temple destroyed it is as if in our day St. Peter's, Chartres and Notre Dame, Canterbury and St. John the Divine all lay in rubble. But you are living stones; you are a royal priesthood, a holy nation. Let society stumble over *you* in your holiness of life. Show it how little the church needs churches, how much God thinks of a people he claims for his own.

The gospel passage is perhaps the strongest of all. Let Thomas question, let Philip ask to see God. Both these challenges have been in place a long time. Jesus is the way to God. He is the truth of God. In him is God's own life. The Father lives in him accomplishing all the deeds and purposes of godhead. Whoever has faith in Christ will do all that he does and more besides. For he is not a man of miraculous deeds and blinding signs. He is a just man, a person who loves.

I read a strong line from the pen of a Mexican novelist in *The Washington Post* two weeks ago. He said of poverty that it is not the will of God but the greed of a few. If that is so the salvation of the world is not the denial of human pain but the love of a few. "I am indeed going to prepare a place for you." That may well be true but we have no evidence of our senses on it. What we know in faith is that Christ is the way to God and that we can walk that way every day.

May 17, 1981   St. James Church

SIXTH SUNDAY OF EASTER
Ac 8:5-8, 14-17; 1 Pt 3:15-18; Jn 14:15-21/Year A

When we speak of ourselves as "the church" we mean we are that community, that assembly in whom the Spirit of God, the Holy Spirit, dwells. In speaking this way we do not claim to possess the Spirit. It is rather the Spirit that possesses us. The New Testament authors were at ease in referring to the Spirit as God's action in all the churches and in individual hearts. This gift of God was distinguished from God in the earliest writings only as name or power. You do not have a clear distinction of the two — God and the Spirit of God — like the unequivocal distinction between God and Jesus Christ. Sometimes even Christ and the Spirit are spoken of indiscriminately. This situation will continue up until the year 250 at least. To be sure, the baptismal formula in the name of Father, Son, and Holy Spirit taken from Matthew's gospel was in use. It ultimately prevailed. But Luke who wrote the book of Acts does not seem to know it and speaks instead of baptism in the name of the Lord Jesus. The gift of Holy Spirit for him is given by a separate, subsequent rite — the laying on of hands.

This is probably related to Luke's theology of the apostles and the Jerusalem church more than anything else. For Luke, everything comes from that hub and center. Peter and John could do what Philip, one of the seven chosen by the apostles in last week's first reading (Ac 6), could not do. As you may know, the imposition of hands and an invocation of the Holy Spirit became part of the baptismal rite at an early date. Much more sensitive for Christian history in what has been read from Acts this morning was the acceptance of Samaritans on

equal terms. This surely rendered the movement suspect in
Jewish eyes. It would resemble the acceptance of Cypriot
Turks into full human community with Cypriot Greeks
today. Any Greeks attempting it in the name of God and his
justice would immediately be suspect as not true Greeks. The
same would be true on the Turkish side. So the Spirit of God,
mysterious as it is, is beginning to show itself in immense
deeds of power. The Greek-speaking Jews, the Hebrew-
speaking Jews, and the Samaritans are all made one in Christ
Jesus. That formula of power seems to have eluded us church-
wide ever since.

"[Jesus Christ] was put to death as far as fleshly existence
goes, but was given life in the realm of the spirit" (1 Pt 3:18).
This does not mean a crucifixion in the body and the glorification of his soul. 1 Peter is a fully Pauline treatise. Hence flesh is
all that marks the old eon, spirit all that characterizes the new.
Christ is alive, body and soul, in the Spirit that has raised him
from the dead, just as we are alive in hope in the Spirit that
was poured out on us in baptism, confirmation, and a myriad
of non-sacramental dispensings. Jesus has ascended to the
Father but another Paraclete is given, a counselor who coun-
sels only truth. Whether we recognize him or not is a matter of
whether we choose to be "the world" or a community in
which he dwells.

Too often for comfort, we people of the church act like the
world. We do not have life because we do not see Christ as one
who has life. Or we conceive life as a possession of the
individual, not recognizing that if one dies — actually dies at
the hands of another — all are diminished.

I received in the mail lately a flyer containing a "Pastoral
Letter on Human Survival." Four Catholic bishops were

among the eighty-six signers who came from the Protestant, Jewish, and Catholic communities. The pastoral is concerned with the threats to human survival posed by sophisticated weapons. "Let us turn from this blindness, this folly, this fascination with death," the letter reads. "Let us proclaim our horror at the neglect of the poor, the violation of life worked in our midst by the sinister presence of nuclear idols."

It is interesting that some of those most committed to the power of the Spirit are little interested in his activity in the human community. Salvation is of individuals, of souls, not of the human race or the globe. I only observe this. I do not deplore it. The phenomenon has a history in Christian life. But to conceive God's action as an exclusively religious matter and not a political one in the broad sense does not have its roots in Israel or the church. That was a later and a not entirely healthy development.

Two weeks ago a governor of one of the states, vetoing the death penalty bill passed by his legislature, wrote: "I do not believe the state should take life because the criminal has done so. I do not believe in deceiving ourselves that the death penalty will solve the problem of violent crime. I do not believe that the ultimate vengeance of execution will make us a better or even safer people. Retribution is not the same as punishment, and official killing is not, in my judgment, a proper or a legitimate exercise of a government." Earlier the same office holder gave as his first reason of several against the death penalty: "It lowers us all as a civilized people."

Whether it be abortion or armaments or legal execution, the death industry helps to destroy the image of God in us. We can not indulge in it in any form and hope to come through retaining the divine life undiminished.

On Thursday we celebrate the living Christ ascended to his Father. "You can recognize the spirit of truth," he said, "Because it remains with you." Does it? "The world will see me no more; but you see me as one who has life, and you will have life."

Perhaps. But not if we choose death.

April 30, 1978   St. Stephen Martyr Parish

SIXTH SUNDAY OF EASTER
Ac 10:25-26, 34-35, 44-48; 1 Jn 4:7-10; Jn 15:9-17/Year B

Memorial Day which we celebrate tomorrow is historically related to the Civil War. There is a song from that war that is especially appropriate to this day though not in the form it took in this country. Here it became, "When Johnny Comes Marching Home Again." It was incorporated into the musical play, "Maryland, My Maryland," and the words are cheerful ones about the reunion of a soldier with his family. In Ireland where it originated the song was one of bitter protest against war. It's title was "Johnny, I Hardly Knew Ye." That is the name of the book of memoirs written about President Kennedy recently by two of his close friends and it has to do with the young, murdered president with a bullet in his skull: *Johnny, We Hardly Knew Ye*. For the lyrics of the song are so direct as to be almost heartless.

> Ye haven't an arm, ye haven't a leg, Huroo! Huroo!
> Ye haven't an arm, ye haven't a leg, Huroo! Huroo!
> You're an armless, legless, chickenless egg

And you'll have to be put with a bowl to beg—
Johnny, I hardly knew ye!

The final verse ends in a way that could sum up this particular Memorial Day very well.

They're rolling out the guns again!
But they'll never take our sons again!
No, they'll never take our sons again!
Johnny, I'm swearin' to ye.

For the first time in a decade this Memorial Day weekend finds our nation not directly involved in a major war effort but the words used to qualify, "directly" and "major," are as important as the statement itself. We are, in fact, bombing Cambodia regularly as a means to get North Vietnam to keep the peace. If that sounds to you like madness it just shows how confused you are over the aims of our peace-loving government. During this past week the president welcomed to the White House all the prisoners of the Vietnam war and their families. It was perhaps the last public act involving these persons who were made so much the focus of attention over the past four years. Senator McGovern said at the time of their release that you might conclude from the President's statements that the war was fought for the sole purpose of getting them back. Their captivity, you may remember, became the reason for continued U.S. war-waging, their freedom became the condition for American withdrawal. Their return signaled the long-awaited peace and was supposed to be some kind of tribute to military wisdom and crafty statesmanship.

One POW, a lad who learned upon his release that his wife was about to leave him, sent regrets to the White House because his new job kept him from coming. Then he lost the job, came to Washington, and found he couldn't get in because all the places were filled. I hope that isn't a parable of the future of these 600 men. The government, aided by the news media, has done everything in its power to convince the country that these 600 were the only ones involved in the war, that they had fought it honorably against the greatest odds and had come home victorious. We have not had our attention much focused on the million-plus veterans, many of whom cannot find jobs. We are not being told a great deal about the 60,000 Americans who died in combat and the thousands of others who died from drugs and accidents because they happened to be in Vietnam. Attention is being drawn only to the 600, most of them high-salaried men taken prisoner while dropping bombs on a nation that for most of the war had no air force.

Hospitals, schools, and residential areas received some of these bombs according to U.S. reporters and international inspection teams. There are still an estimated quarter of a million political prisoners in South Vietnam although President Thieu, a Catholic, piously told Pope Paul when the Pope questioned him directly that there are none — only criminal prisoners detained for plotting against the state. Many of these non-existent political prisoners are Catholics and Buddhists whose crime was opposing all war-waging in their homeland.

We could close the file on Vietnam, honor the last American dead, and turn away from these particular cemeteries forever if it were not for the meaning of our Scriptures. They speak of the love with which God first loved us, the kind of love that makes it impossible for us to be without love for any person. "One who has no love for the brother he has seen cannot love the God he has not seen." There is no loving God apart from coming to terms with the notion of "enemy." But it is around having enemies that the psychological structures of Memorial Day are built. Somebody killed these sons and brothers because these dead were themselves there to kill. They did not ask to inflict death and they did not ask to die. Thus it is that the most ancient patterns of society continue. Thus do we continue to find ways to call by noble names that in each of us which does not love, which allows power and greed and simple ignorance to waste lives.

We need to remember our dead in all wars this weekend. Celebrating war is no way to do it. The only way to memorialize the men whose lives our stupidity and greed have destroyed is to make the lovelessness that war feeds on an impossibility.

May 27, 1973   Our Lady of Mercy Parish

SIXTH SUNDAY OF EASTER
Ac 15:1-2, 22-29; Rev 21:10-14, 22-23; Jn 14:23-29
Year C

The author of the fourth gospel from which we have just read faces one problem in his first twelve chapters and another in his last eight. The earlier part, which many call "the book of signs," selects a few narratives of healing from Jesus' ministry and other matters like his encounters with Nicodemus and the woman at the well to signify that Jesus was truly sent from the Father. He who by nature was from above had come to the home of humanity below to bring those who believed in him back to his Father; but first he must prepare a place for them.

The second part, "the book of the passion," has as its long introduction the discourse at the supper table we have just read from. The final eight chapters, to which a ninth was added by another hand, are concerned to show forth the final, great "sign" of Jesus' life, his crucifixion and resurrection. The evangelist consistently calls this twofold event Jesus' "raising up."

There is a secondary question of importance for John besides this great sign. It is the problem for his late first-century readers of how to carry on in Jesus' absence. You know the terms of John's answer: there is another Paraclete than Jesus (a Counselor?) whom the Father has sent in Jesus' name. It is not as if the Christians had been thoroughly deserted and left with only a memory. They had Jesus' instruction which was constantly being brought to their minds by the Spirit of truth. They also had his "Peace," not the Jewish greeting "Shalom" — as common on their lips as our "Hi" given perfunctorily and without thought — but as the abiding gift of one who will be back. Distress has no place in our lives for John; neither has fear. Life is not a matter of having no Jesus with us or no God. The Paraclete is with us to tell us that Father and Son are together, the Sender with the Sent. Our lives are not meant to be voids of insecurity and doubt. They are pervaded by the Spirit. We are instructed in everything. There is the possibility of peace.

The only proper term for that kind of language is mysticism and we of the West are not mystically inclined. We are men and women of effort and tangible reward. We want our religion — like our politics — to be perfectly clear. But of course religion is not perfectly clear. Only the mentality of the bookkeeper, the lawyer, the judge has made it so. But Jesus was a mystic and John a master of symbol. What we have done is destroy this tradition of the all-pervasive Spirit and the ever-remembered Word and put in its place the definiteness of demand, the precision of practice. The fruit of our infidelity is everywhere evident. The young turn their backs on a mystical tradition — the Jesus tradition — which they never knew as mystical but only as mathematical. They seek solace in the stars which at least, they are convinced, stand for some meaning in their lives. They seek visions and dreams, offered by charlatans and accepted at their peril, because reality has been unkind to them. They look for simple ways of life and dress because the politicians and the educators, the church-men and the industrialists have turned out equally to be liars. The Jesus who gives a gift of peace they have not known —only his local representatives who want to smash commu-nism or not see America lose its first war.

I should not be too gloomy about the modern prospect. The vision of a heavenly Jerusalem lives whenever Judy Collins sings "Twelve Gates to the City" and hundreds of young voices join her. Massive walls like diamonds, foundation-stones on which are written twelve names, three gates east, three north, three south, three west — no problem there. The only problem is that this city of theirs does have sun and moon but above all stars — Pisces, Taurus, Virgo, Gemini. Why? Because the Christian young have not known from childhood a Lamb who was the city's lamp or any light that could be called the glory of God.

The mischief began fairly early, I suppose. Luke's book of Acts records the early struggle in Jerusalem when the action of the Holy Spirit was first legislated, so to say. Paul had first come to know Jesus by way of mystical experience but Paul the mystic lost out and four clear legal prescriptions emerged (Ac 15:20, 29).

Of course, the whole thing was terribly complicated. Up in Antioch the gentiles were being taught that faith in Christ was enough to launch them on a new life. But along came some Jewish Christians from Jerusalem, the capital, who could not imagine how it was possible to believe in any Jew as Israel's Messiah without being circumcised and keeping the whole Mosaic law. It was a familiar case of resistance to something entirely new — as presumably Jesus was. This particular new wine, it was supposed, had to be put in the old bottles of tradition. Paul resisted the whole business. He knew that Christ risen was something different from the way the Jew had always done things, that he was in fact in his own person a new law. But this was not good enough for the earnest Jewish Christians in Jerusalem. They wrote a kindly, understanding letter, setting their new gentile brothers free of obligation —almost. There had been seven "precepts of Noah" so called, which supposedly were binding on the whole human race that did not know the law of Moses. The Jerusalem church, according to Luke, out of all good will and because they could not imagine the entirely new, cut the seven precepts down to four. They thus started Christianity on its path from union with God in Christ to a settlement of reason, a stated way to avoid the divine displeasure. We have been drawn in that direction ever since.

But every once in a while someone discovers the true spirit of Jesus, whether in John's gospel or Paul's letters or the Book of Revelation, and then the fun begins. Such a one thinks that Jesus' word is available in the church, and that the church is all those in whom the Paraclete abides, and that distress and fear have no place in Christian life. All in all, it is a lonely kind of discovery. People think you're a kook. All kinds of unpleasant things happen to you.

All you've got is the satisfaction of being the only kind of believer in Jesus and the Father that Jesus ever showed any serious interest in.

May 16, 1971   Our Lady of Mercy Parish

SEVENTH SUNDAY OF EASTER
Ac 1:12-14; 1 Pt 4:13-16; Jn 17:1-11/Year A

Today is an interesting day in the Christian calendar. We get it from Luke, the man who invented Pentecost. Christian Pentecost, I mean, for as a second spring harvest festival fifty days after Passover Pentecost had a long Jewish history. Since Luke alone reports Jesus' ascension after forty days, he likewise gave us the ten-day interval in the midst of which this Sunday occurs. I am not being frivolous about St. Luke. The other three evangelists deal with Jesus' upraising from the dead as if it were his sole glorification. There, he appears to his friends from his heavenly glory. In Mark Jesus tells them (14:28) — and later the women through a young man at the tomb (16:7) — that they will see him in Galilee. In Matthew he announces to them on a mountain to which he had summoned them (28:16) that he will be with them always (v. 20). At the end of John 21 — this time also in Galilee but as described by a different hand than the author of the first twenty chapters — Jesus says at the lakeshore simply, "Follow me" (21:19). Luke alone employs the symbolisms of the biblical forty days (Moses' time spent on the mountain, Elijah's flight to Mt. Horeb among other examples), then fifty days, to forge a link with the church's parent Israel. We are not a community without roots born instantly once Jesus appeared on the scene. We are a community with roots —deep and abiding Jewish roots. To this St. Luke and the feasts of last Thursday and next Sunday bear abundant testimony.

The prophet Zechariah at 14:4 describes the feet of the LORD — who by definition has no feet — as resting on the Mount of Olives on the day of a mighty battle between Jerusalem and all the nations. By the time Luke writes, the church is calling Jesus "Lord" in a derived sense. It is *his* feet that will stand on a Mt. Olivet split in two, not between north and south as in the prophetic book, not between Jew and gentile, but between those who heed the gospel (Jews and gentiles) and those who do not (Jews and gentiles). That is the tale of an upstairs room entirely populated by Jews, both men and women, who will reach out to non-Jews that most of us are. That mixture did not survive long in the church. Another mixture did: believers like Jesus' plebeian family members and friends, the "ordinary people" of the gospels, and the wealthy women Luke reports who supported Jesus and the Twelve "out of their means" (8:3).

The second reading tells us nothing we have not been hearing from 1 Peter these last six weeks: that to be a faithful disciple of Jesus is to suffer for his name. The passage has a modern ring in that the church's tendency has always been to lick its wounds for non-offenses while failing to suffer in many times and places for the right kind of witness. At the moment, courageous protest is being lodged against the murderous destruction of peoples and the denial of their elementary rights in Guatemala, Nicaragua, Chile, Argentina, and the Philippines. One has the uncomfortable feeling that these situations are being deplored because they are *our* people. I have yet to see my first sign on the lawn of a Catholic church that says "Free Soviet Jews." Yet in light of Catholic history in the Crusades, in Spain in 1492, and in the pogroms of 20th-century Poland, Lithuania, Russia, and Germany — where we were "murderers, thieves, malefactors, and destroyers of the rights" (1 Pet 4:15) of Jews — some small token of redress of balance might be in order. It could be that the current Latin American situation will bring us to our senses, reminding us that we are disciples of a Master who taught justice for all, not just the members of the household of faith. Hence, "suffering as a Christian," as 1 Peter puts it (4:16) ideally means feeling the pain when any other human being's rights are infringed.

Today's gospel, though, is the central piece in our reflections as we come to the close of the Easter season with Pentecost in immediate prospect. The prayer put on Jesus' lips by John in Chapter 17 is at once a concluding testament and a farewell speech — like Moses' song and blessing upon the twelve tribes toward the end of Deuteronomy (Chapters 32, 33). "The speaker [of the prayer; thus Ernst Käsemann in *The Testament of Jesus*] is not a needy petitioner but [Jesus] the divine revealer and therefore the prayer moves over into being an address, admonition, consolation, and prophecy."

"I have . . . finished the work you gave me to do," he says to God, proclaiming his fidelity to the task assigned (v. 4). "I have made your name known" (v. 6). The Johannine Christ has been obedient to his Father in sharing a knowledge of his Father's glory. His obedience has been this very glory incarnated and made manifest. The result of his embassy will be eternal life to believers. Heavenly glory has burst in on the human race with Jesus' teaching. With a knowledge of the only true God and the one whom he has sent we are able to pass from death to life. As Jesus goes to his Father he leaves a portion of the Father's glory behind: the community of faith.

That is a powerful legacy. It has often proved an intimidating one. Fearful of bearing the burden of the glory of God, Christians have taken refuge in a stance of moral superiority or disdain for those who believe otherwise or — desperately —of proving by their unedifying lives that they are really no better than anyone else. Yet all the evidence is that when Christians manifest God's glory as they are called to do they pay the price. They probably know that instinctively and shrink from the pain. In last night's *Washington Star* a columnist spoke of public repentance for national moral fault as the doings of a "born again crew." I suppose it was meant to be a sneer but it struck me as a tribute. I am speaking of the simple awareness that, as a government, we might be capable of grave wrongs. This is now called abjection, self-immolation, flailing. In a healthier time in the life of this country — say a century ago when we did very little of it — it was still called "suffering for the name."

Public morality is a very complex question. So is private. Both can be made to make a little sense in light of the paschal deed that was done for us. In the cross and resurrection God's glory has been made manifest and our terrible need has been laid bare.

May 31, 1981   St. Stephen Martyr Parish

SEVENTH SUNDAY OF EASTER
Ac 7:55-60; Rev 22:12-14, 16-17, 20; Jn 17:20-26/Year C

Three stories of vision are told in today's three readings. In the book of Acts, Stephen sees the glory of God in the heavenly majesty and power of the ascended Jesus. In Revelation — the last chapter, hence the conclusion of the whole Bible — the glory is that of the coming Jesus. The one who ascended is coming soon in glory as "the Morning Star shining bright." In John 17 Jesus has given those who believe in him the glory the Father gave him. He would have them come to him to see the glory which is the Father's gift to him. Thus, the readings present a christology that connects us with the one who lived among us, ascended above, and comes again.

Each celebration of the Lord's day is an invitation in eucharistic symbol to a mystical experience of God. Our words may falter, our song be imperfect, our pace in worship be too fast for contemplation, but we are here for no other reason: to know the glory of God in the man Jesus Christ and in each other. The Lord himself said in prayer:

[To] these [who] have known that you sent me . . .
I have revealed your name, and I will continue to reveal it
so that your love for me may live in them
and I may live in them (Jn 17:25c-26).

I came on something worthwhile lately in a little book by a Lutheran scholar who teaches about the fathers of the church at the University of Notre Dame. St. Gregory of Nyssa, in the fourth century, wrote of God compared to a bubbling spring:

As you came near the spring you would marvel, seeing ,that the water was endless, as it constantly gushed up and poured forth. Yet you could never say that you had seen all the water. How could you see what was still hidden in the bosom of the earth? Hence, no matter how long you might stay at the spring you would always be beginning to see the water. For the water never stops flowing, and it is always beginning to bubble up again. It is the same with those who fix their gaze on the infinite beauty of God. It is constantly being discovered anew, and it is always seen as something new and strange in comparison with what the mind has already understood. And as God continues to reveal himself, people continue to wonder; and they never exhaust their desire to see more, since what they are waiting for is always more magnificent, more divine, than they have already seen (*Comm. in Cant.*, 5:2, Orat. XI, tr. Musurillo and Daniélou, *From Glory to Glory*, 245).

Have you not wondered, sometimes, about the intergalactic movies we are flooded with, the space odysseys that burst on us with every passing week of television to boost the ratings in a sagging season? Special effects do not explain the phenomenon. These are just the medium. The message is that there is the more, the other, the heretofore undreamed of. And the film-makers know the endless thirst to discover it. In these movies the space people are technically superior to the earthlings, but only for the first hour and fifty minutes. They turn out to be very much like the Greek and Roman gods, namely, having all the failings, foibles and jealousies of humanity. Even when creative genius tries to suggest the transcendent in these films, something beyond the mortal or the finite, the attempt ends as somehow flat, ghostly, shapeless. You cannot expect great symbols of God from people not given to constant prayer. In the absence of the search nothing profound is going to be uncovered, not even the faint traces of God. "The force" and the general beneficence of little E.T. turn out to be at root, at base, shapeless. They impel toward a brief warm feeling but not to great deeds.

The poet of Revelation 22 is saying that Jesus Christ the First and the Last, the Beginning and the End is never far from those who hope in him even though he be off in glory. Are you thirsty? Drink! The Spirit and the Bride — Christ's spouse the church and the Breath of God that dwells in it — say to the Root and Offspring of David, "Come!" In a holy impatience believers say to him: "Be with us. The separation is too painful. Come!"

Acts 7 does the same another way. It holds the martyr Stephen in great honor. It knows that only such a one, heavy with human death, can bridge the fault between the human race and God. There has been one of us, says Acts, who has looked upon the Son of Man in glory. St. Augustine said once, in a sermon about St. Stephen, "Let us take the benefits of God through him, our fellow servant."

We long for a set of symbols that will put us in touch with a world unseen, a God unknown who we suspect is all around us. A hundred years ago we could still tell tales of angels and devils, two hundred years ago of the dead who walked the village on certain nights of the year. Recently tales of men and women who zip through the stars absorb us — unaccountable to nature's ordinary laws. Where is power, we ask? Who can do what is right effortlessly, crushing the purveyors of evil? What display of wisdom and strength can reduce chaos to order and let humanity live as it is meant to?

The Christian symbols are simpler by far than all this costly expenditure of cosmic energy. They are first a story told in common and remembered by all, then the semblance of a meal with bread blessed and broken and wine mixed with water poured into a cup. Memorial is made of a past event, present grace is invoked, and a future consummation is anticipated: "Until he come." It is all done swiftly. The foodstuffs are eaten. We reflect briefly, first in silence, then with a common prayer. And all depart.

Our weekly Eucharist is that simple: the community's story read and commented on, its Lord eaten and drunk in symbol. But the thing that gives power to it all is the fact that we are a Spirit-indwelt people, a people loved of whom much is expected.

This family is from Belle Mead, that one from over toward Hopewell. They look interesting. That old gentleman always comes alone, a widower perhaps, or does he have an invalid wife? But none of these details is what makes us matter to each other. It is that we are loved. The Spirit-Paraclete dwells in each of us. We have been prayed for by the one we call Lord before we ever came to birth. He wishes us to be one even as he and the Father are one. Yet Father and Son remain far superior to us, the community, even though the community reflects the divine relationship between Father and Son. Here, unity seems to mean the solidarity of differences.

It is an old and familiar rite we perform. All over the globe it is being done on this day, the Lord's day. The Eucharist is a religious experience for us. It is an opening up of the heavens to give a glimpse of the glory of God, the Alpha and the Omega obedient to our summons, "Come!", a people that knows itself and its God in the breaking of bread.

Pay close attention to that child near you, that older couple, that family, that singleton whose family does not come to church. They are in God and the Son, and God and the Son are in them. Be careful whose hand you shake at the "Peace." He, she, will disclose to you no less than the glory of the Lord which Jesus gave from a Father who gave it to him. In us and over us and through us is the Spirit in whom we likewise dwell.

I sometimes wonder how we can endure all this splendor of godhead in the midst of this blue plastic forest that is our weekly meeting place.

May 15, 1983   St. Charles Borromeo Parish

PENTECOST
Ac 2:1-11; 1 Cor 12:3-7, 12-13; Jn 20:19-23/Year A

There is something like the miracle of Pentecost in modern Israel where the revived Hebrew tongue — long a dead language except for study by scholars of Bible and Talmud —can be heard rather than Yiddish, Arabic or English. In the book of Acts the reversal of the proliferated tongues at the Tower of Babel is suggested. In that ancient story as in Jewish life before the twentieth century there was the division of a people meant to be one. Now there is restoration to unity. The author of Acts makes the subject of everyone's discourse "the marvels God has accomplished" (2:11). This will be spelled out in the passage that follows immediately as the career and glorification by God of Jesus.

We are seven weeks removed from Easter, the time between Passover and *Shabuoth* or Weeks. This was the second spring agricultural festival in Bible times. The Jews of Jesus'

day who spoke Greek called it *Pentēkostē*, the fiftieth day. Two
aspects of the marvel of Galilean Jews speaking in the various
tongues listed are pointed out: confusion and utter amazement
at the marvel and the widespread geographic character of the
Jews assembled. There is no gentile witness yet. The author is
saving that for the conversion of the household of the Roman
centurion Cornelius in Chapter 10. Meanwhile, he employs
the signs of the zodiac to convey universality. Persia (Parthia
in the list) was *aries*, the ram; Syria, *capra* the goat; Egypt
aquarius; Italy (or Rome) *scorpio*, and so on. There are a few
substitutions like Pontus for Armenia and Phrygia and Pam-
philia — provinces of Asia Minor — in place of Hellas-Ionia.
In general, though, the account makes clear that the spread of
the gospel to far-flung parts existed germinally on Pentecost
through the Jews assembled in Jerusalem.

Quite clearly the Christian movement was a Jewish phenomenon in its origins. Yet the power of Holy Spirit was not as
strong a force as the will to division between Jews and Greeks.
Both clung to their customs; early unity of faith in God
through Jesus was lost. God's spirit is all-powerful but it leaves
the freedom of the human will and the force of passion and
prejudice intact.

I spent yesterday — and will do the same next Saturday
—with some lay people of the Episcopal Diocese of New
Jersey doing a workshop on the ministry of lectors. We were in
Moorestown, Quaker and RCA territory, in a church built in
1928 straight out of an English village. Most of the people
present were in mid-life. Many had English names. They were
plebeians, by and large, not patricians. During the day I could
not help thinking of the fortunes of history that had made
these earliest colonists a minority in their own country. It was
not quite as drastic as the fate of Jews in the Christian church

— ejected, for all practical purposes — but there were common elements. On the happier side the Spirit's work has been so fruitful in our day that these readers and chalice bearers clearly belonged to a catholic church. This was far from their story in the colonial founding period. I spent a day in the midst of ecumenism as a reality, not a word or a dream. Fittingly, the consciousness of the impending feast of Pentecost ran very high in the group. It was not just that their reading duties of today had alerted them to it. They were living a life in which the calendar of feasts was central. Ministry for the common good was at the heart of it.

The gospel of John tells of the gift of the spirit in terms much less dramatic than those of Luke-Acts. But it is just as much a reality to this evangelist. The outpouring of divine force or influence is central to the entire New Testament. Spirit accounts for Jesus' equality with God, for his deeds of power. He does not simply die on the cross, he "delivers over his spirit." By holy spirit in power he is raised up from the dead. He gives the gift of the spirit to achieve reconciliation among sinful humans. But, in the speech of the rabbis, the sins of some can be retained; they are held bound. Forgiveness is not complete because there is some barrier. Petitioners of forgiveness are not themselves in a mood to forgive.

Sometimes you hear it said of a person, "He (or she) is a good hater." Christians — genuine followers of Jesus — are poor haters. Their memories of a wound, a hurt, a gross injustice may be as keen as anyone's. They do not cultivate amnesia; that would be unrealistic. But they let God's spirit heal. The Pope's behavior of the last month has been instructive in these matters. His offer to be a hostage in the Italy where he now resides was not an empty gesture but an act of personal courage. He knew the murderous spirit of Aldo

Moro's captors. Their mentality is such that finishing off the Pope would be a feather in their anarchist caps. He stayed close in spirit to the family that was too grief-stricken to extend forgiveness at this time. Most of all, he acted as a healer in the spirit of an Italian people torn by rancor and resentment. He spoke to them sternly and sagely but in no rancorous spirit. The spirit of Pope Paul has been the spirit of God, the spirit of Christ in this divisive, hate-filled period. Heeding the words of Jesus the Pope has distinguished clearly between whom the Spirit forgives and who is held bound, namely those who do not at present seek forgiveness.

Today we celebrate the Spirit's outpouring in full measure on the company of believers that we are: a people warmed, illumined, strengthened, reconciled by a power that far outstrips our own. Like the entombed Jesus we are figuratively a corpse until breathed into by the breath, the Spirit of God.

May 14, 1978   St. Stephen Martyr Parish

TRINITY SUNDAY
Dt 4:32-34, 39-40; Rom 8:14-17; Mt 28:16-20/Year B

If you know the musical *Godspell* or at least its songs, you will recall that the final number is called "Long Live God." As the play is usually staged the rigid body of Jesus — his arms stretched out as if on a cross — is held aloft on the shoulders of a chorus singing the honorific chant, "Long Live God." At first the theology strikes you as bad since the New Testament nowhere calls Jesus God. When a strong tendency in the fifth century did so without enough reference to his being a man, a Galilean Jew, it was stigmatized at the Council of Chalcedon as the monophysite heresy: belief that Jesus had one nature only and that nature overwhelmingly divine. But on second thought the theology of the conclusion of *Godspell* is seen to be like that of John's gospel. There, you remember, Thomas the doubter is invited to put his finger into Jesus' nail-prints and his hand in his side. Upon doing so he cries out in belief, "My Lord and my God!" (20:28). This is of a piece with the earlier statement of Jesus in John's gospel, "Philip. . . .Whoever has seen me has seen the Father./ How can you say, 'Show us the Father?'" (Jn 14:9). For this evangelist the man Jesus *is* the revelation of God. To experience him is to know something of the God no eye has seen. He is the chief sacrament, the primary symbol of God. To be a Christian is to come to know God in Jesus Christ.

Well, do we have in today's feast of the Holy Trinity a feast of the unique divine nature in the spirit of *Godspell* — "Long Live God"? "Praise God above ye heavenly host, praise Father, Son and Holy Ghost"? If we had such a feast it would be unique in the Christian calendar. Our greatest feasts are Christ-feasts — after them come feasts of Mary, the angels and the saints. To pray as believers is to celebrate the way God has shown us the divine power in the only Son, Jesus, and in the Spirit-filled community which we ourselves are. So today's celebration is not primarily a matter of God made known to us in Christ or, through him, in Peter and Paul or Anthony of Padua and Thérèse of Lisieux. It is a celebration of God revealed to us in us. God is triune in the measure that we bear the stamp of the Jesus raised up for our salvation and the Spirit breathing in the church that we are.

We are God's children, Paul says in Romans, heirs by adoption of all God has to give, sons and daughters with Christ the primary son.

Isaac Bashevis Singer, at eighty the winner of the 1978 Nobel Prize for Literature, has delighted countless adults and children with his tales of Polish Jewry in which angels and devils populate the pages as much as Naftali the Storyteller and Gimpel the Fool. Singer tells of meeting a woman at a party who brought him a copy of one of his recently published children's books and asked him to autograph it. "Who is the child?" he asked. "It's for me," she replied, "I am the child."

Anyone who knows she is a child, and whose child, is a mature person.

"Since the Lord your God is a merciful God, he will not abandon or destroy you....Did anything so great ever happen before?...Or did any god venture to...take a nation from the midst of another nation...as the LORD your God did for you in Egypt before your very eyes?" (vv. 31, 32, 33, 34). The Jews of the Bible knew the parent who fathered them. "You received...a spirit of adoption ," says St. Paul, picking up the theme. "Through it we cry out *Abba*, 'Father.' The Spirit gives witness with our spirit that we are children of God" (vv. 15, 16).

Childhood is the one "state in life" that every human being has shared. Each of us knows that there are two persons, living or dead, whose child we are. The dynamics of our relation with that particular woman and man are at work for much of our lives; even if we did not know the one or the other the genetic bond is there. Not all of these relationships with parents are neat and tidy. They evoke strong and often conflicting emotions. Another way of saying this is, it is very hard to imagine being the child of someone other than your own father and mother.

What we are invited to do throughout our lives as believers is intensify our awareness of what it is to be God's children. This calls us to complete dependence yet without a loss of our independence. It can give us total security in a love that will never be withdrawn. This experience of the power and solicitude of the One whose child we are is as intense as our experience of self. We come to know a source where we can be nurtured, nourished, and strengthened without losing our adulthood and self-sufficiency. For it is God who begot us, made us his children and did it through Jesus Christ in the power of the Spirit. We bear the stamp, the imprint irrevocably of the God whose children we are just as much as we do of our natural parents. That is why today is the feast not of the triune God but of us in whom the Father dwells, of whom we would know nothing apart from the Son whom we encounter in a Spirit-filled community. For on our day of baptism we did not receive an incomprehensible formula of words out of Matthew's gospel; we received a literal parenting. With it came an irreversible set of resemblances to the God who begot us.

That is really what today's feast is about. What must this God not be like, the early church asked itself, who achieved in us the marvel of grace that he did? God went out to us twice out of love, once in the man Jesus, becoming the Son we are called to be like, and again in the community that we go to make up as informing breath or Spirit. In what way should we then be consecrated if not "in the name of the Father and of the Son and of the Holy Spirit"? It is the name we bear. The triad of love is the only origin we have. And, as with any family, it is the home we hope to go back to.

June 6, 1982 St. Charles Borromeo Parish

TRINITY SUNDAY
Prov 8:22-31; Rom 5:1-5; Jn 16:12-15/Year C

Juliana of Norwich was a fourteenth-century woman whom you might call a do-it-yourself nun. The proper term is "anchorite," meaning hermit or solitary. But she did not live off in a desert, rather in a cell affixed to the side of a church in a town, where people came to visit her at her window on the world. From there she gave spiritual counsel of the most remarkable kind. The only writing Juliana left us is called *The Showing of God's Love,* a treatise of strongly mystical bent. Here she is, elaborating on a theme from St. Anselm: the reality, intimacy and tenderness of God's "homely loving."

> As truly as God is our Father, so truly is God our Mother; He revealed that in everything, especially in these sweet words where He says: "I am he," that is to say: "I am he, the power and goodness of fatherhood; I am he, the wisdom and loving-ness of motherhood; I am he, the light and the grace which is all blessed love; I am he, the trinity; I am he, the unity; I am he, the great supreme goodness of every kind of thing; I am he who makes you to love; I am he who makes you to long; I am he, the endless fulfilling of all kinds of desires."

We are fated to be giants of the spirit or pygmies depending on whether or not we have a great idea of God. "All that the Father has belongs to me," says Jesus according to John. "That is why I said that what [the spirit of truth] will announce to you he will have from me" (16:15). That intimate friendship with Jesus brings us in possession of God himself is the earliest Christian claim.

That certitude brought the followers of Jesus into difficulties with fellow Jews from the start. I do not mean their claim of intimacy of God, which had long been a Jewish heritage. You hear the first reading from the Hebrew Scriptures in which wisdom is the speaker, the wisdom that was beside God as his craftsman, playing before him daily on the earth, delighting in the human family. The Jew of Jesus' day was exhorted to acquire this wisdom, by fidelity to Torah to come into possession of no less than deity itself. But the earliest disciples, after the resurrection, had a special problem. They had experienced the wisdom of God as a human being, a man in the flesh, and there was no precedent for this in the tradition. Not Abraham, Isaac or Jacob, not Moses, the prophets, or any of the "holy men of deeds" of Jesus' century was thought of as the repository of the divine, "God with us." Matthew used that Hebrew term, *Emmanu-el*, as a description of Jesus. The first followers of Jesus had the quite new problem of describing the intimacy of the risen Christ with God without falling into pagan mythological speech about two gods. They precisely did not believe in one deity who had visited us on earth as the emissary of the other.

God is always God in the New Testament and Jesus is always Jesus, the Christ. The one is not the other. "God, in Christ, was reconciling the world to himself," says Paul (2 Cor 5:19). The work is one work. Those who do it are two, God and the Jew Jesus in whom God intimately dwells. There was, further, a biblical way of long standing available to describe God at work in the world. The term was *ruaḥ* in Hebrew, meaning breath or wind — invisible power, life force. The New Testament translation is *pneuma*, as in pneumatic tire, on which one literally rides on air. In Latin you say *spiritus*. *Spirare* means "to breathe." So God as Spirit became the Christian way to speak of God at work in the world in the community of believers in Christ's resurrection. The second reading from Romans — a letter Paul wrote to convince the community there that he had not betrayed his Jewish heritage — expresses God's work in us very well. God makes us right with him, puts us at peace, through our Lord Jesus Christ. Jesus is the one by whom we have access to grace in *faith*. Through him we have hope that one day the glory of God will be ours. Our *hope* will not be frustrated. We are sure of its promise because the *love* of God has been poured out in our hearts through the Holy Spirit who has been given to us. There is a triad of gifts, therefore — faith, hope, and love —and a triune giver, God through Christ in the Spirit. The new gifts of the Spirit are of unutterable richness. The giver must be equally rich and fruitful, whatever deity in itself may be like.

The course of things thereafter you know something about. Whether, when "the Son" and "the Spirit" were said, the fullness of godhead was meant, or only some creature, some abstract power of God, some manifestation of God in time, was argued out at great length in the fourth century. The conclusions were not inaccurate but were fraught with peril. There were, said church councils at Nicaea and Constantinople, three "subsistences" in God. That is a subtle philosophical word which means that to each of the names Father, Son and Spirit corresponds deity whole and entire, but under a different aspect or interrelation in God's work of redeeming and sanctifying us. Alas, the Greek word for "subsistence" came out as *"persona"* in Latin and three persons sounds like three people. But numerical plurality in deity is the very opposite of what the fourth century church fathers wished to affirm.

Juliana, a thousand years later, has a remarkable handle on the impenetrable mystery of God, using familiar religious language. Notice how much she describes a mystery implicating us, for there is no Christian faith in God apart from the way God's life is ours:

> The almighty *truth* of the Trinity is our Father, for he made us and keeps us in him. And the deep *wisdom* of the Trinity is our Mother, in whom we are enclosed. And the high *goodness* of the Trinity is our Lord, and in him we are enclosed and he in us. We are enclosed in the Father, and we are enclosed in the Son, and we are enclosed in the Holy Spirit. And the Father is enclosed in us, and the Son is enclosed in us, and the Holy Spirit is enclosed in us, almighty, all wisdom, and all goodness, one God, one Lord.

We are fated to be giants of the spirit, or pygmies, depending on whether or not we have a great idea of God. The only God we believe in broods over the creation, plays and sings and dances on the earth, crafting the creation and giving delight. The earth is in our stewardship. The love God has for it calls us to protect it from harm, from war and destruction, from plunder. We were not put here to grow rich and bloated, to prove the superiority of our political institutions by growing rich off others, to express condolences to the bereaved whose deaths we have contrived.

We were put here to preserve the image of God in one another, to be our brother's keeper. We cannot love when we destroy. Dare we even say we believe in the Father and the Son and the Holy Spirit if it means a stern commitment to preserving the face of God in all humanity?

May 29, 1983   St. James Church

CORPUS CHRISTI
Dt 8:2-3, 14b-16a; 1 Cor 10:16-17; Jn 6:51-58/Year A

I have been serving since last fall on a bilateral dialogue, as it is called, between six members of the Catholic Church and six of the United Methodist Church under the co-chairmanship of a bishop of each communion. The latter two are James Malone, Catholic bishop of Youngstown, Ohio, and James Mathews, United Methodist bishop of the district whose two major cities are Baltimore and Washington. We meet twice a year for theological exchange, hoping at the end of three years to produce an account of agreements and differences in the area we have chosen for dialogue which is the Eucharist or Lord's supper.

This meal is a "saving ordinance" for the Methodists. The expectation is that it will be celebrated once a month or even only four times a year. Attendance drops on that Sunday, we have been told, in part because the rite of administering bread and cup — grape juice in the United States, as part of Wesleyan sensitivity to widespread drunkenness on the frontier — is something slow and time-consuming. Also, older American Methodists like older American Catholics entertain feelings of unworthiness, hence abstain. But most importantly the saving ordinance of preaching is so central to Methodist worship that a Sunday without it — as communion Sunday is — is considered a Sunday out of joint, a Sunday lost.

Our United Methodist colleagues — who include the Evangelical and United Brethren, German pietists, through recent merger — assure us that in theory their eucharistic doctrine is that of John Wesley. Wesley remained a priest of the Church of England to his dying day although estranged, from its point of view, because he ordained presbyters, normally a bishop's prerogative. Close attention to the many hymns he wrote in conjunction with his brother Charles reveals a warm-hearted piety that views the eucharistic gifts as Christ's true body and blood shed for us on the cross. One can only agree that the theology of the Lord's supper contained there is Catholic, if of a medieval, passion-oriented kind. But then, our U.M.C. partners go on to assure us, certain Reformation tendencies in theology have been so influential in their church, especially in America, that they do not wish to certify the eucharistic doctrine of all their fellow believers. The spread is wide, they say, from a rich liturgical reform in their church like our own, which has the Lord's presence relative to the elements at its center, to a spiritual presence of Christ where faith in his saving death is central and the symbolism of the meal with its food and drink quite expendable.

Corpus Christi, the feast we celebrate today transferred from its traditional place on the Thursday after Trinity Sunday, is a relic of old religious wars. It is medieval in origin from Belgium and testifies to what can only be called a visual theology of the eucharist. Heretics were denying that Christ was present in his physical form in the bread. Catholics — at the time far separated from the reality of sacrament which of its nature is symbolic — responded by baking gleaming white hosts which they carried in procession on this day. They worked out a theology you know well because you have sung its hymns, which said that behind this veil of bread the reality of Christ was concealed.

Now that may be an attempt to express right faith but it is not good theology. The essence of a symbol is to transmit, to convey meaning, not to hide it. Christ for us is present in a meal of food and drink that conveys the fullness of his serving and loving self. He died for us though we were yet sinners and we make commemoration of that death and subsequent resurrection in a meal that was leave-taking in character. We keep as the bond between us the one loaf, the one cup, signs of our unity as a believing people. If Christ is one and undivided then so must the sign of him be. Otherwise, fragmentation —not unity — will be the Christian, the Catholic reality.

The desert experience, the first reading reminds us, has never faded from Jewish consciousness. There, in the Sinai wilderness, God kept his people with what seemed to them miraculous bread from heaven, while sweet water spilled from the rock of baked clay. The evangelist John did not mean to deny the marvel. What Jew could do so and hope to be heard? He only meant to present a Jesus, faith in whom was greater than the faith of old in manna and gushing spring. To eat of that food was to gain relief but later to face the fact of mortality. To take in the whole reality of Jesus — flesh and blood and all — in faith is to have life because of him. It is to be assured of being raised up on the last day.

I have two friends who are dying at this season. You may have more. They have eaten of this bread and cup many times yet their bodies waste away. I wonder if I should have the faith to proclaim this mystery from this pulpit if I were under similar sentence of death. I hope so. Catholic, Methodist, Christian of whatever sort, this is our faith: that whoever eats the flesh of the son of man and drinks his blood in faith has life within, and will not die forever.

May 28, 1978   St. Stephen Martyr Parish